# It CAN'T Be LUCK

*The Life and Times of Billy Boyd Lavender*

*An Autobiography*

Billy Boyd Lavender

ISBN 978-1-64492-445-7 (paperback)
ISBN 978-1-64492-446-4 (digital)

Copyright © 2019 by Billy Boyd Lavender

All rights reserved. No part of this publication may be reproduced, distributed, or transmitted in any form or by any means, including photocopying, recording, or other electronic or mechanical methods without the prior written permission of the publisher. For permission requests, solicit the publisher via the address below.

Christian Faith Publishing, Inc.
832 Park Avenue
Meadville, PA 16335
www.christianfaithpublishing.com

Printed in the United States of America

# Contents

Foreword ............................................................................................. 5
Preface ................................................................................................ 7
Acknowledgments ............................................................................. 9
Introduction ..................................................................................... 11
The Humble Beginning ................................................................... 13
Sickly at Seven ................................................................................. 17
The Heavenly Orchestra ................................................................. 20
The Incident at Lake Rutledge ....................................................... 23
Too Small to Help ........................................................................... 25
My Great Aunts ............................................................................... 28
Queen Riding High ........................................................................ 30
The Farming Transition .................................................................. 33
Clinton B. Elder .............................................................................. 37
Brice's Pond ..................................................................................... 41
Bobby, the Calves, and Me ............................................................. 43
Wearing Braces ................................................................................ 51
The Band Era ................................................................................... 53
Puddles ............................................................................................. 55
How Not to Rattle Up a Buck ........................................................ 61
Girls in School ................................................................................. 66
Facing the Music, a Forlorn Hope ................................................. 71
Basic Training .................................................................................. 75
Radioman "A" School ..................................................................... 80
Breaking the Heart of an Angel ..................................................... 83
Nimitz Hill Message Center, Guam .............................................. 86
The Antagonist ................................................................................ 91
Letters from Home .......................................................................... 94
The Latter Days of May 1971 ........................................................ 97

June 1, 1971 ..................................................................104
I Met My Heart in San Francisco ................................107
U.S.S. Molala ATF-106..................................................114
Becoming the Complete Radioman............................117
That Music Thing ..........................................................124
Naval Air Station, Albany, Georgia..............................127
Naval Air Station, Jacksonville, Florida......................132
Another Chance at Music.............................................133
The Birth of Joe and My Rededication......................138
One Thousand Records for Promotion......................141
LCU-1661 .......................................................................143
A Strange Occurrence in Palermo, Sicily....................149
Beirut, Lebanon, 1976 ..................................................154
Fishing Patterns.............................................................157
Norwood's Boy...............................................................160
The Seven-Year Plan.....................................................168
Misty Blue......................................................................172
Twenty-One Percent Interest Rates............................175
The Construction Loan................................................184
The Spiral Downward...................................................189
The Heart Transplant Candidate ................................198
A Fork in the Road.......................................................205
The Seed Stock Hobby .................................................212
A Sire for Red................................................................216
Another Talent Show....................................................221
The Donnie Sumner Story ..........................................224
Those Black Little Hands.............................................228
Sitting in the Mercy Seat .............................................231
Forgiveness and Healing...............................................240
Theodore Encounters the Nine Iron..........................247
The Shadow of Death ..................................................253
On Medical Technology's Cutting Edge.....................258
Leaving the Legacy: It Can't Be Luck.........................260
Epilogue..........................................................................263

# Foreword

This is an amazing story of the life and times of an extraordinary man, Billy Boyd Lavender. He grew up with a humble beginning on a forty-acre farm in Northeast Georgia. An undiagnosed heart condition would influence his faith and life. This is a true story about how he met the love of his life, Cheryl Marie Anderson, his high school sweetheart in Watkinsville, Georgia. She would become his wife and faithful companion through the many trials they experienced together.

During the Vietnam War, Billy and Cheryl spent the first few months of their marriage separated by the miles of the Western Pacific Ocean on the island of Guam, a trust territory. He received a top secret special category security clearance and worked in the Nimitz Hill Message Center for the Commander of Naval Forces Marianas Islands. This experience and two tours of duty in the Navy would set forth a career path that is quite remarkable. As a radioman he learned a skill set that would allow him a post-military career.

As a boy, he worked by his father's side and learned to apply the skilled trades his dad was taught at Monroe Agricultural and Mechanical School in 1929. This helped to develop his character and hard work ethic. He learned basic carpentry skills, cattle breeding, and other facets of farming. As a country boy, hunting and fishing were a natural form of recreation.

Billy's faith in God cannot be underestimated. The Lord has a plan for each of us and gives us many talents. It is up to us to develop these talents. He learned early in life of his musical talent, but that was not God's immediate plan for him.

Several times he faced the valley of death only to be spared by divine intervention and support from Cheryl. With each occurrence it became more obvious that God was not ready to bring Billy home. His work on earth was not finished. Breakthroughs in medical technology, considered to be experimental, would make him a candidate at the right place at the right time on more than one occasion.

The strength of prayer in healing is undeniable and obvious. This book reveals how calamity can be just another avenue for God to show his awesome power.

I have been fortunate to know Billy. His story is a testimony to putting faith in the Lord and accepting things will be alright. His story could not have a better title, *It Can't Be Luck*. Thank you, Billy, for sharing your story with us.

Dr. Mark P. Benner

# Preface

*It Can't Be Luck* has been a work jumbled in my mind for a number of years. The issue such as style prevented me from taking on the task sooner. Another issue was the religious overtone of the work that could be viewed as uninteresting to many readers. On the other hand, those class of readers may well be the target audience.

Convinced that this book is a work the Lord has led me to write; it has taken some time to decide upon the style and delivery that would make it interesting and different from the standard autobiography. Also, it has taken time for these events to occur in my life. After they occurred, it further confirmed that it should be my witness as a Christian and my legacy. All Christians have a testimony and the majority are similar. Also, I have discovered that no matter how difficult the trials in my life have been, there have always been some Christians who have been affected differently and left with much deeper feelings on the subject.

Discerning the will of the Lord can be confusing without referring to his word to help clarify the direction that each Christian should take. If a Christian is also gifted with many talents, the directions can become numerous which can also add to the uncertainty.

The kindling used to ignite these dormant thoughts was gathered on a trip with my church's Fun and Travel Club. Sitting across the table from a few church members at dinner, the conversation seemed to hit on something that I was familiar with or had actually experienced. I tried not to dominate the conversation, but it turned more toward an interview as my friends inquired more about each topic. I realized at that point I should begin this work and be diligent to ascribe all glory and honor to my master each time he powerfully intervened in my life.

Another note of encouragement came from the officer in charge at my last command in the Navy before I was discharged. He wrote in my last evaluation that my oral and written expressions were both excellent. That observation was not equally noted by all my superiors throughout my eight years of military service. During my first enlistment one evaluation read I was "loquacious by nature." It was pleasingly apparent at the time of my discharge the way I expressed myself had improved.

With the aid of related graphics, the vignette style of writing affords a type of expression that gets to the point quickly when so many topics need to be covered.

# Acknowledgments

At age forty-one the director for the Center of Heart Failure at Emory University Hospital, Dr. Andrew Smith, gave my wife and I the grim news that I would die of congestive cardiomyopathy if the clinic did nothing. I was put on the heart transplant list after three months of testing. While I waited on a matching heart, I was tested by the clinic each quarter in an effort to find a way to save my life. Nine months into the testing, it was discovered that I was a candidate for a new procedure that few surgeons in the world could perform. It was not an exact science at the time, and I became the fifty-first patient in the world to receive a partial node ablation of the interventricular septum by laser. It was successful, and I was removed from the transplant list as my heart began to strengthen.

In 2002, a horrific automotive head-on impact occurred with apposing "G" forces in excess of 120 mph. My wife and I were critically injured. I was given a 20 percent chance of survival, and my wife was expected to be in a wheelchair for two and one-half years. We both were divinely healed.

The long-term effects of the blood thinner, Coumadin, created a slow brain hemorrhage that was confused as vertigo by four different doctors. On Christmas Eve of 2015 the "still small voice" inside me spoke clearly. "This will kill you if you don't go to the ER." I lost consciousness immediately after registering at St. Mary's Hospital. I awoke on life support in their ICU. After another long stay in ICU, I was rehabilitated and returned home with no lasting ill effects.

I would like to acknowledge my Lord and master, the Great Triune God, for his abiding presence with me through the "valley of the shadow of death" on no less than three known occasions. As the psalmist further wrote, "For thou art with me, thy rod and thy staff they comfort me."

# Introduction

Mark Twain was quoted as saying, "The twentieth century is a stranger to me." For many older Americans the twenty first century may be viewed the same way. The bonding of my immediate family began during the Great Depression. It seemed everyone in America was at some level of poverty financially. For the rural family, in many cases, the more important necessities of life were faith, adequate food, shelter, and clothing.

My parents were great providers, having benefited from the wise instruction of their recent ancestry. My great grandmother contributed immensely to their success. She was ninety-one years of age in 1940. She was a teenage girl at the end of the Civil War. Her wisdom and experiences were invaluable.

A reporter for the *Athens Banner Herald,* Wayne Ford, once wrote:

> Billy Boyd Lavender's mother died in October of 2014 at age 96. She welcomed the opportunity to tell stories, Lavender said. "I took a recorder and was able to get the details down." Lavender said he began writing in the early 1970's when he became a communications officer in the U.S. Navy aboard the U.S.S. Raleigh. The chaplain of the ship read his first efforts to write about his family and heavily marked his manuscript with edits, Lavender said. But while he pointed out many mistakes, the chaplain told Lavender that he enjoyed reading about his family, which remained a source of encouragement.

The word *talent* in scripture is a curious word with a dual meaning. Its definition applies both to money and value as well as skill and natural ability. Perhaps both meanings should be inseparable. To the many Christians who have few talents monetarily, they may indeed be very talented. Christians also believe they receive these talents from their creator. The scripture is clear in addressing how we, as stewards, should use these given talents.

Jesus explained, "To whomever much is given, of him will much be required; and to whom much was entrusted of him more will be asked" (Luke 12:48).

In Matthew 25:15, he explains, "And unto one he gave five talents, to another two, and to another one; to every man according to his severability; and straightway took his journey." Upon the Lord's return he will ask for an accounting of what he has given to us, his servants. To the one who received five talents and made five more, the Lord said of him, "Well done good and faithful servant." To the one he gave two talents, the same was done, and the same reward was given. The servant who buried his talent and did nothing with it received condemnation and rejection.

Christians view their lives as a spiritual pilgrimage. "For our struggle is not against flesh and blood, but against powers, against the rulers of the darkness of this age, against spiritual host of wickedness in high places" (Ephesians 6:12).

It is important for me to leave this autobiography of vignettes as a legacy. I am a miracle recipient many times over, and my accounting for what he has done in my life must be shared.

With this introduction I invite the reader to look over my shoulder. The reader may distinguish how my life has been made different by one of servitude and divine intervention instead of stardom. After reading this autobiography, they may discover the attributes of my Invisible Friend and how they are intertwined into the great love he has for each of his creation.

# The Humble Beginning

I remember the early days of my childhood with great fondness. In the 1950s and eighty-five years removed from the Civil War, there still remained much change to take place with civil rights legislation. But for me, under the walnut trees in the backyard pushing my toy tractors around in the sand, now that was the most important issue of the day. It was a faster-paced lifestyle in the 1950s than when my dad was a kid in 1914, but likewise, the 1950s were lived at a much slower pace than today.

Instilled in me were the ways and means of a day gone by. The stories of fodder, mules, and two-horse wagons were imprinted in my imagination and psyche. Many other traditions were carried over out of necessity such as hand milking at least two cows, making butter, and killing at least one hog during the coldest day of the year. One of my favorite excursions with my dad was taking selected wheat from the field to the mill on the creek. There the old water wheel turned tirelessly as its cups were filled over and over with an endless stream of water. I remember the noise of the water and those large millstones grinding together and was startled when the mill operator stepped out of the entrance covered with flour from head to toe. Inside the mill was the smell of flour, and like the operator the powdery dust was on everything.

I was blessed by being a country boy and raised in a fine family with six members where everyone was older than I was. My dad was born in 1909, and my mother was nine years younger than him. They raised four boys, Roger, Jimmie, Bobby, and me. Unlike many Americans who moved from house to house, state to state, and church to church, I never knew but one home and one church for the first nineteen years of my life. All during those years, I took for granted the grand old church and community of Antioch. Not until I had visited many different countries in the Western Pacific and the Mediterranean did I awaken to the call of home to once again surround my family with the same community and church that had been such a valuable blessing to me.

Though I do not remember it, in 1951 my great grandfather, a man of considerable wealth, came to the tin-covered sharecropper's house at the Big Springs Place. It was there the rest of my family was living when I became their last member. Mother's grandparents' house, the Hardigree-Haulbrook house, belonged to Lula Haulbrook, an only child. Subsequently, when Lula died, my great grandfather, Phillip Hardigree, held only a child's interest in the farm, and his children held the controlling interest. In 1951, after Phillip's family had left the nest, the house became vacant, and Phillip decided to rent it out. But his eldest daughter, Aunt Trudie, confronted her father, saying if anyone was given an opportunity to live in the house, it should be his granddaughter, Ruby Neal, her husband, Clifford, and their four small children. So on this day, after some deliberation, and while Dad was still working at Dairy Pak in Athens, Georgia, Phillip paid a visit to my mother.

Hesitantly he said, "Hmm, hmm, if you and Clifford want to work the Haulbrook farm on halves with me, I'll come down with my truck tomorrow and help you move."

There was no way to notify Dad of the good news, so Mother immediately began packing for the next day's move. So in 1951, the Hardigree-Haulbrook house became a home for our family. For the next ten years, Dad sharecropped with Phillip and paid rent, which left very little from the annual farm income. If there was any livestock production over that from a single milk cow, a hog, and a few chickens, Phillip expected to receive half.

The forty-acre farm was a splendid place for an adolescent boy like me to grow up. There were numerous outbuildings including the privy, and there was no running water in the house. It was a home where dashing through the snow took on a literal meaning during inclement weather. My favorite chore with Mother beside me was finding hen nests with several eggs in them. The chickens did not always lay in the row of nests Dad made for them. We had to find the nests and retrieve the eggs before the old hen started to set and brood her clutch.

Hardigree/Haulbrook House

# Sickly at Seven

Growing up as a healthy male human being is truly a wonderful and amazing state for anyone having attained to that status. The feelings of invincibility run parallel with it, and he never thinks of the future perils or possibilities. If the young could look into the future and see what lay in store, many would say as I would have said, "No! Not for me!"

To see me today one might never know how concerned I made my parents in the early going. It seemed I could not quite get a grip on some sort of normalcy with my growth. The big house was hard to keep warm in the winter months with just wood heat; thus, I would alternate from one sickness to another. The sicknesses ranged from the common cold to influenza, and Mother would come to believe I once had a touch of rheumatic fever, if there could be such a thing. Now looking back on that and the serious health issues I have subsequently encountered, I supposed it is possible.

The doctors at that time believed my health would improve if I had a tonsillectomy. The day came for my operation, and it was one I shall never forget. As I remember the moment they rolled me through the double doors into the operating room, the nurses pounced upon me. My face was smothered with an ether-soaked cloth. When I gasped for breath I drew ether into my mouth and nose. I know that I struggled, but soon I went under.

Two or three days back home after that hospital trauma, I wondered how such a bloody ordeal could make me feel better. The blood clots were gross, and I seemed to produce them in great quantities. In another week or two, that area in my throat healed, but I still did not have an appetite. It was another visit to the doctor, and this time I was given a clean bill of health. All that I needed was vitamins.

The doctor recommended a thirty-day supply of once a day multiple vitamins, and that was all it took. My appetite returned, and soon I was back on track with my growth. I did not get sick so often either.

Looking back on this period of my life, I experienced much improved health, but I believe some subliminal damage had been done. I personally believe it was about this time I acquired a lifelong antagonist, atrial fibrillation. The symptoms of the nemeses would always visit during periods of excitement, and it would manifest itself with a fainting spell. I suppose everyone has fainted at one time or another, but I fainted more than my share. After I would have a fainting spell, the nature of the affliction allowed my heart to revert back to a normal rhythm so quickly it could not be diagnosed. I lived with it untreated for thirty years.

In 1960 it was not uncommon at the Watkinsville Elementary school to, on occasions, walk down School Street with the teacher, to the downtown area. The county seat of Watkinsville had a small County Health Department in 1960. On this field trip of sorts, the entire fifth grade class took this trip to visit the county nurse, Mrs. Marsh. She listened through her stethoscope to each one of our hearts. When my turn came she took a little extra time and started to ask me questions. She was careful not to alarm me, but I was impressed enough to remember that she remarked, "You must be an excitable person."

It was not uncommon for my brothers and me to get into all kinds of mischief. On a farm in the early 1960s, there was plenty of harmless mischief to come our way. With nothing but a pair of cutoff dungaree shorts, I was chasing a bantam chicken through a hog lot barefooted when I came to a screeching halt. A ten-penny nail in a board that lay beneath the surface of the mud went through my foot. I screamed to the top of my lungs.

My elder brother, Jimmie, who was seventeen at the time and outside the pen heard me and shouted, "What's the matter?"

"I stuck a nail in my foot!" I cried back, as the blood gushed in the filthy mud.

Jimmie was hesitant to jump in the pen and wanted me to pull my foot off and come out. I may as well have been tied there with a steel cable.

"I can't! Help me!"

My appeal must have sounded desperate, and he reluctantly entered the mess and jerked my leg and foot free. The bleeding was profuse. Jimmie carried me to the house, and Mother cleaned me up.

I am not sure if it was the same day or not, but very soon I was back at the doctor's office for a tetanus shot, and a *drain* was placed in the wound. The nail had penetrated the thick part of my right foot between the base of my big toe and the next largest toe. It nearly broke through the skin on the top of my foot. A dark bruise just below the skin could be seen on the surface. Later, as it healed, a scar formed there. It is still visible today.

I was bedridden for over two weeks so the drain could do its job. The drain eventually worked its way out, and the wound healed over.

# The Heavenly Orchestra

Sometime around 1958 while all the brothers were still at home, a strange and very personal phenomenon happened to me. Our blue Chevrolet pickup truck was still relatively new. It was a plain truck with no accessories. It had no radio, no air conditioning, power windows, etc. Dad and all of the boys were packed onto its single seat. It is not clear to me why it was the five of us or why Mother wasn't with us, but because of the space limitation I was tucked under Dad's right elbow as he drove the truck. I remember that I had dozed off.

It happened when Dad awakened me. In the moments between slumber and consciousness as I awoke, I heard beautiful music. It wasn't like the country music Mother and I listened to on the radio at the house. It wasn't church music. It really was like nothing I had ever heard in my short life. It was such a wonderfully strange occurrence I asked Dad and my brothers, "Do you hear it?"

"What?" They replied.

I said, "Shhhhh, listen!"

No one heard anything, but for me it was a soul-stirring event.

I have referred back to that moment as the origin of my musical talent. It was as if a switch had been thrown to activate something deep in my genetic makeup. It was presented as a talent to be used for the giver's purposes. It would take a lifetime for me to understand its implications, its ramifications, and its usage.

I practiced my talent privately. I knew something had happened that changed me differently from what I had been. My voice would change with puberty, but the talent was still there. Once while chopping cotton behind Jimmie and Bobby, I joined in with them with full gusto on a song they were singing. They looked back at me in surprise. I was embarrassed, but I noticed their nod of approval. I began imitating the singing cowboys, Gene Autry and Roy Rogers, and other country and western singing stars in my privacy.

Prior to 1958, Antioch only held services once a month, and the entire family would pack themselves into the Chevrolet pickup and attend as often as we could. This afforded Mother up close and personal inspections on how well we had bathed. She looked for what she called rusty spots behind the ears. She would take a handkerchief and wet it with her tongue and nearly rub the skin raw in such places.

Antioch Christian Church is the oldest of its denomination in the state of Georgia. Every August the old church holds its annual revival. The many members that it has welcomed into its fellowship over the past two centuries have come by way of profession of faith during this week of refreshing sanctimony. Mother began asking me questions of a spiritual nature, and in turn I had a few for her. This was the time when children of my age were expected to make a decision.

The revival of 1960 was no different from the many it had held before. My friend, Wayne Marable, and I sat in the very first pew at Antioch and sang at the top of our lungs, so much so the preacher even commented on our spiritual fervor. The appropriate time to approach the preacher and make a profession of faith in Jesus Christ was at the end of the service when the invitation was given. I did not fully understand all of what it meant. All I knew was I could now participate in taking *communion* like the big folks. Now, no one had to worry about my eternal destiny because I was a Christian member.

I don't really know what I expected to happen after I was baptized. I tried to do the right thing. I tried reading the Bible, but it seemed a little hard for me to understand. I prayed in a childlike manner expecting something like magic to happen. I still had to be disciplined, like before, but there was one noticeable difference. I noticed it when I would wander down the dusty roads of home by myself. When I was alone with just my BB gun late in the cool of the still evening, I would practice my talent. The crickets would start to chirp with the song of the whip-poor-wills. With the pungent fragrance of honeysuckle in the air, there would be a wonderful calm to come over me. I could feel my heart pound. It was at these times

I felt a presence and a peace I had never known in such a way. The biblical scripture that I learned later was, "Be still and know that I am God." I sought out this time alone with him as often as I could, and he never failed to meet me or forsake me, though many times it was I that turned away from him.

# The Incident at Lake Rutledge

In the early 1960s it was not uncommon for Mom and Dad to take short trips on Sunday afternoons for a picnic. Once we were at Rutledge State Park on such a picnic. The lake had a swimming area with a water slide. I could hardly wait for the recommended hour to expire after lunch before going into the water. Mom and Dad did not swim but spread the blanket on the beach area and watched me splash around.

The other kids that were my age were having a blast sliding down the huge waterslide. I failed to calculate the length of the slide and the depth of the water at the end of it. The ladder to the top of the slide went up about twelve feet. After getting permission to try out the slide, I became a bit apprehensive when I reached the top, but the other kids were right behind me, and so there was no turning back. I really did not know what I was in for as the slick wet slide took me down much faster than I had ascended. I remember my back was flat against the slide as my body jettisoned across the surface of the water like a skipping stone. I had not learned to swim at that point in my life, and I disappeared beneath the surface of the water.

Dad had been watching from the beach area and saw me disappear. I was literally in way over my head as I floundered around in six feet of water holding my breath. I did not know which end was up. I was very disoriented a considerable distance from the bottom of the slide. Everything about "swimming fun" was over for that day as a strong hand grabbed my tiny forearm and pulled be above the surface.

As I caught my breath, I could see Dad, fully dressed, splashing into the water near the slide. His shoes, socks, and pants were wet above the knees reaching out for me and yelling to the Stranger at the top of his lungs. The Stranger's grip was firm and strong. He lifted my fifty-pound body with one arm and in a single motion swung me into the arms of my father. I had not noticed the Stranger before I slid down the slide nor did I see him afterward.

Later that summer at Daytona Beach, Florida, I learned to swim in the motel pool.

# Too Small to Help

About the time of my puberty in 1962, my voiced cracked at the breakfast table. It seemed strange to me that I could not control how I said things. More times than not when I spoke, it came out normal, but with increasing frequency it had a deeper tone. In an effort to keep it the same, I deliberately spoke in the deeper tone, which sounded funny to everyone in the house. I was beginning to feel the effects of the chemical changes testosterone and the growth hormones were having on my physical body.

Mother was working at the Snow White Laundry branch office and providing the extra income that our family needed. She purchased a new bedroom suit to furnish the company bedroom. Our old house had not been remodeled, and the wooden porch had obvious holes in its deck. The furniture store delivered the items Mother had purchased to the back porch where they were crammed near the kitchen entrance. As Mother and Dad took each item into the upper room, as we called it, there remained one last dresser and mirror. I knew they were getting fatigued and asked if I could help. Dad said no. He explicitly told me not to touch the dresser until they were ready. I thought I would surprise them if I did it all by myself. I intentionally disobeyed my father in hopes the greater good would show him how strong I was becoming. While they were in the upper room, I worked first one end and then the other toward the entrance. The leg at one corner went through the unseen hole in the porch. Try as I might to upright the top-heavy dresser, it crashed to the floor breaking the large mirror.

I knew I was in for it and had to face the music. I knew what was coming, so I took off my belt, took it to Dad, and handed it to him. He looked bewildered. I thought he might go light on me if I would be honest. I told him I had broken the mirror. He lashed me from the upper room down the hallway into the living room and onto the porch. When he saw the broken mirror, he continued the lashing down the steps into the yard between the hedges until I was under the porch.

Three things happened that day. (1) As long as I lived in that house, I did what he said. (2) I never again volunteered my belt. (3) It was the last whipping I ever received from him. As my brothers left the nest one by one, my dad and I grew ever closer and worked together with pleasure and harmony.

The big house was cold in the winter months. It had five open fireplaces and three chimneys. We burned a lot of wood. The WD Allis Chalmers tractor had a power takeoff that ran a belt pulley flywheel. Dad put a wide belt long enough to reach the front of the tractor where he mounted, upon two timbers on each side of the tractor, a sawmill saw blade. The saw blade was about three feet in diameter. Wherever Dad could find wood to burn, we would go there and saw it up. Tree limbs and sawmill slabs were the predominant source for our heat. This was labor-intensive work, and Dad knew the importance of canvas work gloves and high top boots. What a difference in the ability to work and stay warm with all our extremities protected.

After we were tucked in our beds with heavy quilts over our heads, we would often let the fires go out. Even under the covers when the bottom fell out of the thermometer it was cold. We soon discovered a simple remedy, the electric blanket. Wow! What a modern marvel! In the winter it was not nearly so hard to go to bed, but it sure was difficult to get up in the mornings.

Living on the forty-acre farm, our family observed many of the old-time farming methods. Because of Dad's agreement with Phillip, little improvement to the house and out buildings was risked. Dad was not financially able to make these improvements while we rented. If Dad did make the improvements, Phillip might not have renewed the agreement between them and would seek better terms with another sharecropper at our family's expense.

Eventually our family was given the option to purchase the farm and an additional one hundred acres nearby when Phillip and my grandfather, Ralph, died just months apart. I felt privileged to work, live, and hunt on the same land my ancestors had owned. It was prime for small game and deer hunting, and that suited me just fine.

# My Great Aunts

The children of Phillip Hardigree were the immediate heirs to his fortune. His fortune was comprised of the many acres of land to which he acquired ownership after purchasing the timberland. The reciprocal benefit of selling the timber and paying for the land left him with vast acreage throughout Oconee County. Though he left an inheritance to his grandchildren, it would require that they wait for twenty-five years after his death for the timber on a particular tract of land to mature.

Phillip's first wife, Lula Haulbrook, was the only heir to the forty-acre farm and the Hardigree/Haulbrook house. Different inheritance issues were arranged when she passed in 1929. The forty-acre farm was left to her immediate family. That meant Phillip only held a child's interest. In that course of events, all of Phillip's children left the nest, and the large house became vacant. "Taking a page from their father's book," Aunt Trudy bought up enough of her sisters' and brothers' parts to have controlling interest in the farm.

Most of Phillip's children had a different vision for how the forty-acre farm should be rented and operated. This brought about the ultimatum from Aunt Trudie to her father, Phillip. If anyone was to live and work on the vacant farm, it should be our family if we wanted to live there.

This love and concern for my immediate family from my mother's aunt created a special bond between her and the rest of Phillip's children who were like-minded. Consequently, my Great Aunt Trudie, Great Aunt Ebby, Great Uncle Lester, and my Grandfather Ralph became very close to my dad and my mother in the subsequent years following Phillip and Ralph's death in 1960. Because of the disputes in the inheritance matters, my mother's aunts and uncles became just as close to my family as Mother's brothers and sisters.

Aunt Ebby married a wealthy entrepreneur named Luther Suttles in Americus, Georgia. After 1957 when we purchased our first automobile, we visited their family many times. They had a boy and a girl, James and Sandra. James was more of my brother, Roger's age, and Sandra and I were the same age. They lived in the suburbs of Americus, Georgia, on several acres, and owned a sprawling brick house. Sandra had two horses. On one visit in 1962 Sandra saddled them up.

Sandra's purpose for having horses was to show them in Western Pleasure and Trail Horse events. Sandra's two horses were Blaze and Prince. They both were properly trained gilding trail horses. I looked forward to visiting Sandra so we could ride the southern back roads around Americus.

On a horse ride in 1962, I asked her if we could race them. She seemed to have some reservations about that but said we could canter them for about a quarter of a mile. I knew nothing about horse terminology or what cantering meant, so I followed her lead. When she told her horse Prince to "get up" with a slight nudge with the back of her heel, they were off and running. I did the same. Up until that day in my life it was the most exhilarating ride on anything I had ever experienced. With each bound of the length of the horse it was as if we were in the air flying. The wind whistled in my ears as Blaze's mane flapped before me. The speed at which we were riding went from a boring walk to about thirty-five miles per hour. The trees and fence posts went by so fast we covered the distance in short order. It was the shortest but most unforgettable ride I had ever experienced. That memory was etched into my soul forever. I had a special love for horses from that moment forward.

# Queen Riding High

Jimmie was working at the A&P grocery store in Athens one cold winter's day in 1959 when he heard the whimpering of a puppy beneath a car in the parking lot. He felt sorry for the little puppy and brought him home to the farm. We named her Queen, and she became a member of our family. She appeared to be part collie by her markings. She had short hair, and the rest was mutt. She was plenty smart and proved to be talented. She was quite faithful and followed Dad to the fields and would follow behind the four-disk tiller Dad was plowing with until her tongue would hang out from exhaustion. Once when Dad had stopped, she rested in the cool plowed dirt under the disk tiller. When Dad started to plow again, he heard her yelp as he turned her under. It cut her hind foot severely. It maimed and disfigured it, but it healed up OK.

    She would follow the truck wherever and whenever it went to the fields. It was hard to break her of the habit since most of the travel was on the farm. But on occasions we would have further distances to travel, and she would still follow. On those occasions we put her on the bed of the truck and gave her a ride if it was more than a mile or two. She liked her newfound status and began to jump on the truck whenever we moved it. At times when the truck was loaded with fertilizer, there would be no room for her to ride except high on the fertilizer stacked to the cab. That was OK with Queen. It was not too long before she was quite literally riding high. When the truck was fully loaded with fertilizer, we had no way of knowing at times if she was with us or not. She just took it upon herself to pay attention and not be left behind.

    Once we were on Highway 15 loaded with fertilizer, and every car we passed would throw up their hand as if to say hello. We thought it was funny, so we waved back. It was not until Queen stepped off the cab of the truck down on to the hood did we realize they had been pointing to Queen riding on the cab.

After a while she would step down from the hood to the fender of the pickup to bark at all the dogs that would chase our truck barking at her. "Woof!" "Woof!" "Woof!" They would fiercely go at it, snapping and barking at each other. Sometimes their mouths were just inches away from one another. After the dogs stopped chasing the truck to our delight and hers, Queen would hop back to the hood from the fender and take her position like a giant hood ornament. It did not matter which end of our 1950 Chevrolet pickup she used to mount the truck. When we came to a stop or used the truck brakes, she would back up accordingly until her hind end pressed hard against the windshield giving us a very undignified mooning.

During one of the last years we planted cotton, we were chopping cotton down the long rows in front of the big house. At the end of these long rows was an old house place grown over with honeysuckle. Ahead of us about fifty yards Queen was barking furiously at something in the honeysuckle. The closer we got to her, the more intently she barked until she yelped and withdrew with a rattlesnake attached to her nose. She shook violently to free herself from its grip, but that only caused more venom to be injected. She disappeared for the rest of that day. When she reappeared, she was swollen so badly she was hardly recognizable. She almost died, but after a day of two she was able to swallow a little bit. After that incident she was very sensitive about where she stuck her nose.

Feed for the livestock was everywhere on our farm and so were the large wharf rats. They were our number one nescience on the farm. They not only ruined large quantities of the feed, but they would also ruin corn by shelling it off the cob to get to the soft heart of the grain. They also gnawed holes in the feed sacks. They burrowed beneath the ground and gnawed holes wherever they wanted to go. For every rat seen in the daylight, there were fifty burrowed out of sight. Queen would sniff them out, and she inevitably was bitten on the tip of her nose right where the rattlesnake had bit her. She shook it free but immediately pounced back upon it and resumed the rapid shaking and crunching until the rat's fatal demise. Queen hated wharf rats, and so did we. Dad paid me $.25 for every rat I killed with our .410 shotgun. One evening after sundown, I taped a flashlight on the barrel so I could see how to shoot the nocturnal creatures. I took my dad a five-gallon bucket full of dead rats.

Queen was one of a few farm animals/pets that lived out their lives on the farm. She came to us in the early 1960s and left us after all the boys were grown and gone.

# The Farming Transition

Some major changes were about to take place. The big house was built in 1908, and little had been done to preserve its stately beauty. Over a half century of deterioration was becoming obvious.

Soon a representative from the Farm Home Administration came to our house and recommended that Dad borrow enough additional money to build a poultry house to pay for the farm and make improvements. Dad took his advice, and, slowly, things began to change. With this better life, we were back to the farming grind more than ever, just to be able to afford it. I was growing big enough to help significantly. I even drove the pickup truck around the farm if Dad needed me to do that. I lifted fertilizer, slopped hogs, and fed 11,500 chickens with two five-gallon buckets that were emptied into forty feed troughs.

When Dad discovered that our broiler house was kept warmer than the big house by its gas brooders, he invested in gas stoves for each room in our big house. It was wonderful.

Dad still row cropped some, but the steady cash flow was the income from the ten thousand capacity broiler house. By the time I was thirteen, my three elder brothers had left the nest. The farm chores now rested squarely upon Dad and me. After I got off the school bus, I would eat a snack and join Dad in whatever he was doing for that day. Sometimes it meant going straight to the fields. Other times there was a routine list of chores that needed to be done.

In November of 1963 while in junior high school, I sat with my classmates in a math class. Each classroom at Oconee High School was wired to an intercom system. The terrible news came over the speaker that President Kennedy had been shot in Dallas, Texas. We all waited anxiously to hear further news of his condition. It seemed like forever, but it wasn't long, the news came that the president had died. At that very moment the fall wind stirred briskly outside the opened windows. The small replicas of the Georgia State flag and the American flag blew over on the table in the front of the classroom; Mrs. Smith allowed me to set them upright again.

Because I had been allowed to drive the truck in the fields, I thought that it was OK to find Dad and to drive there. He had driven the tractor and tiller to the Howard Ward place about two miles away. We were renting the acreage from Aunt Ebby, Phillip's youngest daughter. The way to the Howard Ward Place was by country dirt roads. When I arrived, I could see Dad plowing upgrade on a high bank near the road. We saw each other about the same time. I stopped in the middle of the dirt road as he approached. He shut down the tractor and looked down at me in the truck from the high bank.

"What's the matter?" he said.

I said, "President Kennedy has been assassinated."

Dad dropped his head in silence and disbelief. He paused for about fifteen seconds pondering what to do. Then under his breath, I heard him whisper, "There's nothing else to do but go home."

Dad left the tractor right where it sat and scuttled down the high bank. I scooted over to let him drive home. I told him what I knew about it, but we mostly rode in silence. After we arrived at home, Dad turned on the black and white TV. My dad sat in front of the TV and watched the national news for the next several days. We watched the drama between Lee Harvey Oswald and Jack Ruby play out on live TV. The farming chores halted for about a week. Bringing in the firewood to warm the November chill was the extent of our activities.

For Christmas of 1963 I had asked Mom and Dad for a new twenty-six-inch bicycle. What Santa actually brought was a twenty-four-inch bicycle. I tried not to show my disappointment, but I did comment that it was too small. Just the same, I fell in love with it right away. It was a new shiny red machine. When I sat on it, I looked like a fully grown man on a donkey. Nevertheless, when I raised the seat and the handlebars, it fit me fine, and I was the master of it right away. I went everywhere on it, and I think Dad liked it too. He saw right away how fast I could get around the farm without taking the time to walk. He was always giving me errands to run. It was a real exercise tool also. I was growing rapidly with the good food I was eating. My height and weight increased from about 5 ft. 1 inch and 110 pounds at age thirteen to 5 ft. 9 inches and 150 pounds by the time I was fifteen.

Mom, Dad, and me

# Clinton B. Elder

Our farm was located in a corner where two dirt roads intersected Highway 15. The Kirkland Road bordered our front yard. Elder Bridge Road formed the other part of the dirt road intersection of the highway. Elder Bridge Road cuts across Oconee County through what was once Elder, Georgia, to the Antioch Church Road. Joseph Elder had three wives and fifteen children. The Elders moved from Virginia and settled in the area that formed Elder Bridge road in 1807. It is not surprising that Elder, Georgia, had its own post office, and the Elder descendants made their home all along this road frontage.

My grandfather, Ralph Hardigree, bought a 150-acre farm on Elder Bridge Road in 1930, a mile from where the Elder's Covered Bridge crossed over Rose Creek. In the early days, before buses, my mother walked with other children to the car pool that would take them to school in Watkinsville. The children would cross through the covered bridge on the way to Shannon Elder's house and their car pool destination. The first house on the left and up the hill was where Doc and Frances Elder had lived before they were murdered. Their bodies had been thrown beneath the covered bridge, which made the children's trek to school particularly spooky. Mother and the other children would run as fast as they could through the shadows of the bridge to reach the other side. It takes very little imagination to hear the rapid patter of the children's shoeless feet echoing in the dim lighted bridge.

In 1963 Bee Elder occupied the house that Doc and Frances Elder had occupied. Bee Elder, a black sharecropper, and his family lived next door and sharecropped with Shannon Elder. Bee's family consisted of his wife, two boys, and two girls. He was a small black man, but he worked hard and was a successful farmer. He supplemented his farming income by selling quality, non-tax-paid, corn liquor.

In those days I rode my bicycle in all four directions from the intersection. After I had pedaled a quarter of a mile from our home, the surroundings were interesting and refreshing as if I was taking a trip to a far-off place. It was on one of my bicycle rides toward the creek when I first met Clinton, Bee's youngest son.

He was a small boy but almost as old as I was. I had often seen him before, walking barefooted from the intersection, toward Jimmy Thomas's store a mile down the road. On Elder Bridge Road, I had an opportunity to meet him and strike up a conversation. We became friends immediately. He told me he was going to the store to get something to eat. I thought that was a long way for him to walk, just to get something to eat.

I empathized with him and said, "If my bike had another seat, I would give you a ride."

Having no extra seat did not bother him. He was fine with that idea and offered to ride on the handlebars. I had seen that done before, but I had never done it.

He showed me, however, by straddling the front wheel and reaching backward with his hands, he firmly grasped the handlebars just below my grip. With a quick hop his buttocks fit squarely between our hands. His legs dangled on both sides just for a few seconds as I held our balance. He then curled his big toes around the spindle that protruded past the lug nut on each side and then said, "Let's fly."

I was aware of how my driving was affecting his comfort, so I avoided as many ruts as I could and stayed in one of the two hard-packed tracks of the dirt road, which was as smooth as pavement.

For two centuries, before Highway 15 was paved, sections of the old road between Greensboro, Georgia, and Watkinsville would wind back and forth tracking the high ground for the two horse wagons and buggies. The Highway Department surveyed it straight for the higher speed traffic and effectively cut out the old curvy dirt road. About one-fourth mile below our house, the old road veered off the pavement and proceeded another three-fourth mile distance to the store. With a few hundred pumps of the pedal, we arrived at Jimmy Thomas's store.

True to his word Clinton went to the pastry shelf and retrieved two "honey buns" and asked Mr. Jimmy for two pint cartons of chocolate milk. To my surprise Clinton paid with a $5 bill and then took his purchase in a sack. I thought a $5 bill was a lot of money. We were then ready for our return trip.

A few hundred yards from the store on the old road near the shade of a tree Clinton said, "Stop here." He hopped down, reached into the sack, and pulled out a pint of chocolate milk and a honey bun and gave them to me. There we sat on the bank and had the first of our many picnics together. It started a trend. Almost every time we met after that, he would say, "I'll buy if you fly."

It did not take long for me to figure out where Clinton was getting his generous allowance. The cash flow in Clinton's family was substantially larger than our family's cash flow. It was most likely from Bee's secondary income. Dad also figured this out. I don't know if Dad's pride was showing through or if it was the current events of the civil rights era, but he suggested that I not ride Clinton to the store anymore for the fringe benefits. He said, "Folks will talk about you!" In my way of thinking, if that was all my dad was concerned about, it did not bother me at all.

Often, I would meet Clinton at his house before he had walked anywhere. One such time I quietly rode into his yard on my bike while everyone was inside. As I looked around for someone to contact, I saw Bee just for a moment, as he was about to cross over a terrace in the cotton field near his house. I saw clearly that in each hand he had two plastic gallon milk jugs filled to the brim with some sort of clear liquid. It could have been water, but when he dropped to a squat and then rose up empty-handed, I knew it must have been White Lightning.

I acted as if I had seen nothing. He called for Clinton, and we continued on with our adolescent schedule for the day. It was some months later before I told him about what I had seen. I only did this because I wanted my friend to know he could trust me. He loosened up some and then told me more than I wanted to know. He did, however, explain why his older brother, Paul, always drove a fast Chevrolet Sedan with heavy-duty shock absorbers in the rear end. All of what he told me was verified when Paul was caught by the county sheriff with a boot full of liquor.

Once I met Clinton leaving his house with a cane pole and a can of worms. I was unaware of any place to fish nearby and asked where he was going. He looked at me with a puzzled look and said, "The creek!" That was the first time in my life that I realized Rose Creek had fish in it big enough to eat. I always thought creeks only had minnows. I was about to learn differently.

Directly below Elder's Covered Bridge, the cascading shoals flowed down the moderately steep glossy rocks to a large rock in the middle of a pool at the bottom. The large flat rock could not be seen from the bridge. The water frothed up there with white foam around the edges as the water split and ran by either side of the rock. To get to the flat rock, we walked down a slick path on the steep banks of the creek. At the bottom we hopped from one rock to another to get to the rock island in the middle of the pool.

The water was rich with oxygen from the naturally aerated falls, and the pool area was teaming with small fry. Every freshwater fish imaginable was collected there: blue gill, hornet heads, blue catfish, channel catfish, mud catfish largemouth bass, warmouth bass, carp, suckers, etc. They were not very big, about six inches long but edible. Almost immediately Clinton started pulling them out one after another. A naturally dished-out spot in the middle of the flat rock had filled with water. It was a natural live well and kept the fish fresh until we were ready to go. In a few minutes Clinton had as many as he wanted to clean and then let me try. The pool would furnish up to twenty-five or thirty per fishing trip, but its inventory restored rapidly.

Something permanent happens to a boy when a fish gets hooked on his cane pole. I could not get enough of that feeling. Something unseen below the surface pulled mightily and bowed the pole and straightened the line. I became an avid angler from that moment forward for the rest of my life.

# Brice's Pond

The land directly southeast of our forty-one acre farm belonged to Brice and Sara Downs. More often than not as I traveled the dusty Kirkland Road in the late afternoon and evening, I would meet them much in the same way I met Clinton. They only had one daughter a few years younger than me and no sons. In some strange affectionate way, I think they accepted me as their own son. We became close friends and neighbors.

The property line that separated the two pieces of land ran along the headwaters of Wildcat Creek. The spring at the head of this small tributary was on our property but meandered back on to the Down's land. Several hundred yards downstream, the head of another small creek headed up on our side about thirty feet from the line. The landscape on Brice's side was perfect for a two-acre farm pond.

He and Dad discussed the possibilities of the pond construction. They agreed that the backwaters of the pond could act as a water hole for our cattle, so Dad granted him an easement, and Brice built the pond. Brice stocked the pond with blue catfish.

While the small catfish fry was growing, the pond became the home for hundreds of bullfrogs. Their croaking could be heard a mile away, and I often went to sleep from the sound of their drumming. I talked Brice into taking me frog gigging in his boat early one summer evening. It was tremendous fun for a scrapping fourteen-year-old country boy. The blue cat population became unbalanced, and Brice decided to seine the pond and restock.

Seining was an exciting and muddy mess. We caught tubs full of two- and three-pound catfish with our bare hands. Everyone involved was covered from head to toe with black muddy silt. Brice restocked with brim and largemouth bass, which maintained a more natural balance. He did not want any fishing in the pond while the small fry was growing.

During the summer of 1965, I began to notice just under the surface of our watering hole schools of fish. They appeared to be about three-fourth pound yearling bass. I had graduated from the cane pole to a cheap Zebco 202 rod and reel. At Jimmy Thomas's store where I bought ammunition for my rifle, I noticed some artificial rubber worms with flashy little paddles attached to them. I bought a pack of two and tried them out on the bass.

I lost the first plastic worm when the bass struck it so hard it stripped it off the line. I did not know how to tie a proper knot. Brice Downs was the first man to show me how to tie on a hook. I never used another method for the rest of my life. Mom and Dad had gone to Louisiana to visit Jimmie, and Bobby and I were left at home. I caught about six bass for a private fish fry while they were gone.

# Bobby, the Calves, and Me

My closest sibling, Bobby, is five years older than me, but in 1965 we were about the same size. He had finished Georgia Southwestern Junior College in Americus, Georgia, and transferred back to the University of Georgia. His plan was to work the summer months and graduate from the University of Georgia, only nine miles north of Watkinsville. One of the conditions for his acceptance into the university was for him to commute. Since Mother's daily work destination was close to the campus, it was an amicable situation.

Jimmie, my second eldest brother, had decided to make the Air Force his career. He was stationed in Cambodia during the first half of the Vietnam War. The rest of Jimmie's family came to live with us while he was away. The east side of the big house had two fireplaces, two closets, and three rooms. It was easily converted into an apartment with a bedroom, a living room, and a kitchen. The boy's bedroom that was once ours became part of the apartment for Jimmie's family.

Bobby and I moved upstairs. The upstairs of the Hardigree/Haulbrook house was one large room. The stairway entered the middle of the room with protective railings around it. It was furnished with two double beds, dresser, desk, table, stereo, and the gas heater, which made quite a cozy existence for Bobby and me. There were double windows looking south over the farm and a single window facing north up the highway.

As an older sibling, Bobby was more financially stable than I was. We were able to work out agreements between us. There were some things Bobby could afford at age twenty-one that I could not at age sixteen. He is still a close brother, and I love him and all he did for me.

At times when short jobs would present themselves, Dad would allow me to work them to make a little cash. The jobs varied from working in a peach orchard punching cards for the pickers to working for my uncle Carl on the dairy. Uncle Carl's work ranged from hauling hay to cutting grass. Uncle Carl was financially well off. I was disappointed when the time came for him to pay me and I did not receive cash.

The first time I worked all day for Uncle Carl, I cut his large yard on his riding lawn mower. When it came time for my pay, he brought me to the gate of the corral by the dairy barn. There on the ground beneath its mother's feet was a scrawny jersey calf. He pointed to it proudly smiling and said, "It's yours." It weighed about forty pounds. I tried not to show my disappointment, but looking back, it was the beginning of an era. He and Dad must have talked it through before I was made aware of it, because what was I going to do with a calf?

I adjusted and fell in love with the cute little bovine right away. At the time I did not know much about cattle bloodlines and genetics, but this was a purebred Jersey heifer. Uncle Carl would use a Jersey bull to raise a few replacement milk cows. By using Jerseys, Uncle Carl could better regulate the proper amount of butterfat in his milk product. Holstein cows produced a higher volume of milk but with less butterfat. I took the small calf home and named her Bossy.

The next time I helped Uncle Carl, I was paid in kind with Bossy's half sister and the next time a Guernsey. We were making good use of some of the outbuildings on the farm by turning them into stalls for my growing herd.

When I was a small child, Dad sold "B" grade milk. He was noticing the interest I was showing in raising these calves and decided to work out an arrangement with Uncle Carl on a larger scale. We would grow replacement heifers on halves.

Dad made the agreement to raise thirty-six heifers to weaning size, about two hundred pounds. He would furnish the stock, and we would furnish the feeding and labor. Eighteen of them would be ours, and Uncle Carl would take the rest back to the dairy farm and raise them to breeding age.

Naturally Bossy and my two other heifers were a few months older than the other thirty-six. That meant they bred and calved before the others became old enough. Bossy was taken to a neighboring farm and left for a while until she was bred to a shorthorn bull. She calved nine months later. Dad and I had to pull the calf to assist Bossy who was approximately six hundred pounds, which is small for a cow. However, her confirmation as a Jersey milk cow was phenomenal. She had a dark dished face with glossy black symmetrical horns that curled sharply inward. The rest of her body was fawn colored, and her udder was huge. Dad allowed me to keep the proceeds from the small calf crop that I was able to produce with these first few heifers. This allowed me to have a means to negotiate deals with Bobby.

Bossy and the other two heifers were trained to the halter. Before we had a pasture, I would stake out my calves wherever I could find good grass for them to eat. As Bossy grew to breeding age, I would wrestle with her like a cowboy bulldogging a calf in a rodeo. With both of her horns grasped with my hands, she would try to lift my weight, and sometimes she succeeded. Most of the time I just slid across the yard as she pushed with all her might. This concerned Dad because Bossy's horns were sharp.

The next year Dad turned the land he had row cropped into a forty-acre pasture. We put an electric fence around it and turned our twenty-one heifers onto it. The single electric wire would short out at times. Once the whole herd escaped onto the highway. The traffic was zipping up and down the road and blowing their horns. Dad was worried they might cause an accident and called me to assist him in rounding them up and driving them back into the pasture. Try as we might, some would go one way and some another way. When we both were nearly exhausted, I suggested that we call Bossy. Dad thought for a second and told me to bring a bucket of feed. Dad rattled the bucket, and I called. Bossy came straight to the feed, and the other twenty followed just like schoolchildren right behind their teacher. When we closed the gate behind them, Dad made a vow. He said this to Bossy, "Old girl, you have a home as long as you live." He kept that vow. She raised a fine calf every year and died of old age on the farm.

After the farming chores were completed every day, Dad turned his attention toward home improvements. From 1964 to 1965, Mother, Dad, Bobby, and I put in our fair share of time on a multitude of projects ranging from painting, installing a bathroom, plumbing, wiring, landscaping, new porches, etc. Dad's post-educational schooling in the 1920s included attending school with Uncle Carl at Monroe A&M. There he received vocational training in carpentry, mechanics, masonry, and agriculture. I saw Dad apply these skills many times while growing up and working by his side.

My first year in high school afforded me the opportunity to join the Future Farmers of America. This membership was offered during the agriculture class taught by Sammy Sanders. Agriculture classes were considered easy, and all the teenaged boys liked it because it was all male participation in 1965.

Oconee County, Georgia, in 1962 had four elementary schools. They were located in the communities of Carithers, Bogart, Bishop, and Watkinsville. The students in these locations were graduated into junior high school for the eighth grade at the new high school built in 1957. This created a vast number of new friends and classmates that frankly we hardly knew existed. In 1963 about one hundred thirteen-year-old students were schooled together as classmates for the first time for the next five years of high school.

In Sammy's agriculture class in 1964, the young boys from all over the county became more acquainted with each other. One redheaded, fun loving boy was to become my lifelong best friend. Sitting by me in the agriculture class for the first time was John Michael Marable, Wayne's younger brother. Before class began I noticed his strange behavior. He was using the sharp point on the blade of his pocketknife to prick the tips of his fingers. He had a small vile of alcohol he used to moisten the tips of his fingers and then resume the pricking. Of course I asked him what he was doing. He said he was making the tips of his left fingers calloused. When I asked him why he was doing that, his answer intrigued me. He said, "So when I play the guitar, I can play it better, and the tips of my fingers won't hurt." The intrigue deepened and so did our friendship.

Mike and I had much in common. We both went to Antioch, and we both loved hunting and fishing. For the first ten years of our lives, we lived in a dilapidated house. In our case the big house had redeemable qualities. But the Marable family was able to build a fine new brick home. I thought my good friends, Mike and Wayne, were very fortunate. I visited more at Mike's house than Mike visited at ours.

At school in the fall of 1964 Sammy Sanders handed out a complicated-looking query that was several pages long. Sammy had planned to take some of the agriculture class time to have his students fill it out and turn it in. He did not plan to take the entire class time. The query was on home improvement. It seemed to me every item on the document was about something I was familiar with, my hand kept popping up for clarification. Sammy slowly worked his way to where I was sitting and began looking over my shoulder. He was somewhat doubtful I could have done all these projects. I admitted to him I did not do all these things alone, but this was the very reason I was not involved in more extracurricular activities at school. My services were needed at home. The query represented a possible five hundred-point perfect score. I scored 485. Whatever else Sammy had planned for the class that day had to wait. I barely had time to complete the form.

My teenaged life was a busy one, and Dad was aware of the importance I put upon my time alone. When Bobby was twenty-one, he ordered at my request, a single shot .22 rifle from the Sears Roebuck catalogue, and I paid for it. Except for maybe the bicycle, that was something I had wanted for a long time. I kept it with me when I walked alone down the dusty roads of home. I blinked at everything and often would bag a young rabbit for breakfast or supper.

Sometimes my off time was spent with Mike at his new home. I was impressed with Mike's ability to play the guitar. It seemed to run in his mother's family, and Mike's Uncle Buck had even played on the radio. I knew if I could learn to play I could better accompany him and myself when I sang. Mike soon realized he could teach me better if I too had a guitar.

Mike's neighbor, Mrs. Laura Shelton, had a guitar just like the one Mike had. She agreed to sell it to me for $5. I did not have $5, so the two of us set about seeking a means by which I could make enough money to purchase it. A local peach orchard in the Apalachee community was looking for teenage help to punch the peach pickers cards for each basket of peaches they emptied into the wagon. That was just right for what we were seeking, but we had to have our Social Security numbers. We went together to the Social Security Department and received our numbers, and like our close friendship over the next fifty-three years, our SSNs were in succession, inseparable by not even one number. Mike secured the job for the two of us so I could buy the five-dollar guitar under Mrs. Laura Shelton's bed. We practiced together and marveled at every milestone of our achievement.

Though Dad was amenable to my visiting Mike, he was a bit skeptical of all the time I spent at Mike's house practicing. One evening when I was at Mike's house and needed a ride home, I reluctantly called Mom and Dad for that ride. They, also reluctantly, came for me. To ease the tension, Mike and I put on a miniconcert for both sets of parents. To my delight, my parents were impressed, and from that moment forward, Mom and Dad became our most avid fans.

My Invisible Friend and I walked in the evenings quite frequently, and I sang to him. More often than not, I sang the hymns I had learned in church. On occasions I would try imitating the country and western singers I had heard over the radio. Remembering the lyrics to songs came particularly easy for me. I felt more empowered after my walks alone in the evenings, and nobody knew or ever heard me sing. I was later to learn it was a spiritual gift from my Invisible Friend, and he would jealously guard it and direct my use of it for his glory.

Bobby continued with his schoolwork, and Dad and I continued with the farmwork. Dad and I were chopping several acres of cotton on land he had rented for cultivation two miles down the highway. I don't know why we ever left the house without filling our water jug, but we did. When the late spring sun raised overhead to about eleven o'clock, Dad and I became thirsty. I tried to persuade him to let me drive the truck home and fill the jug with ice water and return. For some unknown reason, he was particularly adamant about doing that himself.

I chopped on alone getting more and more thirsty. The time came and went when I thought Dad should have returned. He had taken more than an hour for an errand that should have taken fifteen minutes. When Dad arrived back in the field, I stood on my hoe handle and stared at him as he approached me with the water jug. He was grinning. I was not. Before I could speak he said, "Wait a minute! I can explain everything." A representative for the Home Improvement Award Program had come to inspect our home to see if the query I had filled out was legitimate. Dad had given him a tour. When I pressed Dad about what the representative said about my chances of winning the contest, he said that the man commented, "No other participant even came close."

I won a trip to the National FFA Convention in Kansas City, Missouri. I would be one of ten thousand students from around the United States who were recognized for their achievement in the organization.

# BILLY BOYD LAVENDER

Braces 1966–1968

# Wearing Braces

Two decades before the unprecedented popularity of the orthodontic surge between 1982 and 2008, more adolescents were beginning to wear metal hardware in their mouths. This conglomeration of stainless steel wires and metal became commonly known derisively as braces.

When I returned home from the National FFA Convention, my sophomore high school pictures were sent home for our parents to select the ones they wanted. Frankly there wasn't much from which to select. Never before had my natural smile been more compromised than when I was fifteen.

Around the supper table, I often became the topic of conversation among the three of us especially now that Bobby was away in school. Some of my classmates had worn braces on their teeth for years starting around the age of twelve after most of their permanent teeth were in place. At age sixteen my complicated mouth had become full of teeth with no room to grow. My mouth was very crowded in 1966.

Wearing corrective braces was becoming more socially accepted, but I wasn't convinced. Nevertheless, Dad would inspect my mouth regularly before or after supper. Mom and Dad talked about how to finance a regular visit to the orthodontist. With Mom's income from Snow White Laundry and Dad's two poultry houses, they decided to send me for consultation with an orthodontist.

They were still unable to financially afford both upper and lower correction and decided if they could just improve my smile that would be enough. Several of my upper and lower permanent teeth had to be removed before the orthodontist could start.

So at the beginning of 1966 I began to have my teeth extracted in advance of having braces applied to primarily my top teeth. After I healed from the extractions, I was ready to start. To properly straighten my top teeth, my bottom jaw and teeth became part of the process and required anchor bands around the remaining bottom molars.

In retrospect the financial sacrifice my parents provided during this important part of my development was an example of their love for all of their boys. It expressed how much they wanted all of us to succeed in life. Dad would have to spare my help on the farm at least one day a month. Being able to drive myself to the orthodontics helped out. I could ride with Mom to her work and then use the car for the appointment. Sometimes I was excused from school in the afternoon to go to the orthodontist.

As a note of encouragement, Dr. Williamson always complimented me on how clean I kept my teeth. He once asked me if I would be an example for several of the patients he had seated for adjustments. I agreed not knowing what it meant. He walked me in front of each of the seated patients and asked me to give them a big smile. He would say, "That is how I want you to keep your teeth!" The shiny stainless steel against the pearly white was about the best part of my smile.

During the middle part of my senior year in high school, I had my braces removed. I could not stop smiling all day long. They were so smooth and white my tongue could actually slide across my front teeth. My bottom teeth were still somewhat crowded, but as planned my smile was corrected.

# The Band Era

High school rock bands were common in the mid to late 1960s. If you were fortunate enough to put together a decent band, a teenage band member could make a little money, not to mention the improvement of his or her popularity status. Gigs for "Sock Hops" were easy to get almost anywhere. When Mike purchased a Les Paul electric guitar and amplifier, I had to have an electric guitar also. It was time to break out the Sears and Roebuck catalogue again. The top of the line in the catalogue was a red "Silvertone," hollow body with three pickups, six switches, and a waver bar. It was a beauty for $215.

I worked out an agreement with Bobby. He could have the proceeds from the sale of one of my calves if he would order the guitar for me. It was a deal. It seemed like forever waiting on my electric guitar and amplifier. I was hoping it would arrive in time for the High School Junior Variety Show so I could participate with it. David Hardigree and I played in the FFA Band, and we had a spot in the show. David and I were to perform an instrumental called "The Girl from Ipanema." David picked the lead, and I was to assist him on rhythm guitar. I would have to use my box guitar if my electric guitar did not arrive in time. My new guitar came in the night of the show. It was so pretty and shiny we just had to use it. Neither David nor I was used to it, and that did not help our performance at all. David wanted to play my new guitar, and I let him, and I used his. We performed OK, but we did not have enough time to familiarize ourselves with the difference in each other's instruments. I'm sure that had some bearing on the results.

The FFA Band was absolved in 1965, as its members sought membership in other bands whose repertoire contained more rock and roll dance music. Mike and I were at times in the same band, but I mostly liked country music, which hampered my skill in the more rambunctious rock and roll. I felt more comfortable playing if I did not act so wild to the extent that it was needed to be successful with rock and roll. My Invisible Friend was becoming an ever-abiding witness to my conscious.

I thought I would form my own band so I could have more to say about its direction. We named our band "Mother's Little Children" and practiced regularly in the empty rooms across the hallway. My parents tolerated the noisy practice sessions. We performed in Athens at different venues, but the band did not have the cohesiveness necessary to bond together. Only one member later played professionally, and he moved to Nashville.

I took a part-time job at the Puritan Cordage Mill on Barber Creek. I drove our old 1957 Ford to and from work. Our newer family car had become a 1964 Chevrolet Impala. Mom and Dad had taken over the payments on my eldest brother's automobile when the Navy unexpectedly shipped him to Scotland.

# Puddles

In 1966 Mike Marable inherited a trained bird dog named Judy. His Uncle Seab wanted Mike to have his wonderful companion. He knew that Mike would hunt her and keep her active. She was an Irish setter and English setter mixed. She looked like what you would expect. She had shorter hair than the typical Irish setter and a smaller frame. She was red with a few spots of white on her. She was smart. She was housebroken and performed special tricks like bringing her feeding bowl to you when it was empty. She pointed and retrieved.

Mike and I enjoyed hunting quail with Judy. She was an equal opportunity collector of quail. Mike and Wayne had double barrel .16-guage shotguns. When Mike and I hunted, I used Wayne's .16-guage because it was more practical than my single shot .410. Judy used her paws. Once after an incredible point, the birds flushed, and Mike and I each shot twice. We downed three birds. Mike and I picked up two of the birds while Judy sniffed out the wounded bird. When she flushed the wounded bird, she knocked it from the air with her front paws and retrieved it.

Jerry Peck, one of our classmates, had a full-blooded male Irish setter. Mike bred Judy to Peck's sire. The result was surprising. The litter had three black puppies and three red ones. Peck chose "pick of the litter," and Mike then got his choices. Mike kept one black male and one red female. They were beautiful. The physical characteristics were that of the Irish setter, long flowing glossy hair and large frame. The black was supposed to have come from the Llewellin setter that was used in breeding up the Irish setter. Whatever the reason for the black results, Mike was partial to his red female which he named Ellis. Mike blamed his black puppy for interfering with Ellis's training and scolded him harshly to which the black puppy responded by tucking his tail and wetting. Therefore, he was derisively named Puddles.

When Mike deemed his two puppies could no longer work beside one another, he asked me if I would like to have Puddles for my own. I jumped at the chance. He was a handful at four months of age. It was obvious that Puddles would grow into a large, beautiful, shaggy Llewellin setter. I estimated his weight to be about forty pounds at four months.

The moment I put Puddles in the old 1957 Ford, he began to communicate to me as much as I did to him. He was a hipper puppy and wanted to run everywhere he went. He had no collar or leash, so I thought I would put him in the boot just for the ride home for his own safety.

When I arrived at the house, I opened up the boot to find a trembling four-month-old puppy frothing at the mouth with white saliva. I was so sorry for my ignorance. It was at that moment I realized I was dealing with a super sensitive dog. That was the moment that I decided to reverse the training trend from harsh to gentle, very gentle. Puddles responded remarkably. He started to look to me as his master for everything. It was so obvious that he wanted to please me. The only thing he wanted in return was for me to treat him with kindness and gentleness.

Dad started to grow turkeys on halves with Hot Thomas as an experiment. At that time local turkey growers were doing well, and Dad was between contracts and gave it a try. Hot was adamant about getting rid of Puddles right away. He thought because he was a bird dog he would raise havoc with the turkeys. Dad did not know but sided with Hot because Hot had more turkey experience than himself. I promised to keep Puddles under control, and for the short term he could stay.

Puddles's house broke easily. He heeled almost everywhere we went except when we were training. I would let him go then, and boy could he go. With the slightest gruffness in my voice he would respond and watch me to see what I wanted him to do. I would point in a direction and whisper an encouraging word or two, and he would be off and gone, instinctively zigzagging fifty to seventy-five yards in front of me. Sometimes in his exuberance he would overrun robins on the ground, and other times he would point them so perfectly I would let him hold the point until I flushed the bird. Though robins were not the game we sought, I figured Puddles was smart enough to figure that out as he gained experience. I rewarded everything he did perfectly with love and kindness, and the tone of my voice did the rest.

I was late coming in from a date one night and kicked my shoes off across the upstairs bedroom. I undressed as I made my way to the bed. The next morning Puddles had held his bladder as long as he could stand it. He started pawing at my shoulder and the mattress. I finally gave in when I realized what he wanted. I sat up on the edge of the bed scratching my head as I tried to wake up. I first put the shoe on nearest the bed and was looking for the other. I was not moving fast enough for Puddles. He sniffed out my other shoe and brought it to me and dropped it by my foot. He led the way down the stairs and out the kitchen door and through the screened door on the porch, down the steps, and squatted only inches from the bottom step. I had to laugh at his persistence as I reflected on the previous few antics he had performed.

Puddles's training was moving along at an accelerated pace. At about six months he pointed a robin so perfectly I took him a step further, flushed, and shot the bird. Puddles kept his eye on the downed bird that had fallen in Brice's pond. Puddles stood at the edge of the pond whining at the fluttering bird in the water. I had put on rubber boots up to my knees. I stepped into the water up to the tops of my boots and encouraged Puddles to come in and retrieve the bird. Courageously Puddles first tested the water and then jumped in and swam to the downed bird. His big paws hit the water, plump, plump, plump, until he was by the bird. Then with remarkable precision, he clenched his teeth on the last quarter inch of the bird's longest wing feather and swam from the lake and gave it to me. The only thing improper about that training method was it is illegal to shoot a migratory bird like a robin. But it was worth the risk for the wealth of experience Puddles gained that day. I vowed the next time I shot it would be the real thing. That is when we started hunting in earnest.

Fall approached and so did quail season. Puddles and I went out for a day of bird hunting. He looked bewildered when I would walk by everything he pointed that was not quail. I felt sorry for Puddles because he was trying so hard to please me. Finally, our opportunity came. I could hear and see the quail chirping and scurrying on the ground up ahead. They ran into cover just before Puddles caught wind of them. Puddles locked down on a beautiful point. It made me grin. As I approached behind him, I encouraged him to get closer, and he responded by moving in like a stalking cat. As we inched closer to the quail, they finally became unnerved and flushed. I shot and missed. Oh well, it wasn't Puddles's fault, and I praised him with everything I had. "Good boy!" I said. He was getting the idea. The explosion and the smell of gunpowder, quail, and the noise of the flushed covey, I'm sure, stuck in his mind. He was less than a year old, and he was displaying awesome potential.

By the time turkeys were taken from our poultry house to be put on a prepared feeding range, all turkey growers had over one dollar invested in a single bird with an additional dollar every week they were on the range. The time was fast approaching when we would put several thousand turkeys outside.

That preparation meant Hot would put poison out for predators like coyote, fox, and bobcats. This phase would only take a week or two, so I made preparations to board Puddles with my great uncle Lester's bird dogs for a while. I asked Dad to be sure to let me know when Hot planned to put out the poison so I could move Puddles off the farm. That did not happen, and Hot showed up unannounced and commissioned Dad to help him distribute tainted hamburger with arsenic. I was in school that day.

When I got home that afternoon, Puddles was not up. Dad was unusually quiet. He told me that they had put out the poison. I became angry. He said he tried putting him on the wagon for the ride home, but he jumped off and ran beside the tractor and wagon. Dad said he caught wind of something in the air and went back in the direction of where Hot had put the poison. Angrily I told Dad that he had a phobia for riding, and he could run three times faster than the tractor. I told him again that Uncle Lester was fine with boarding him for a while.

Puddles did not come home that evening. After a sleepless night, I dressed for school the next morning and waited for the school bus. The moment I left the screened porch, I saw by the well, lying motionless in a running pose was Puddles, dead. The school bus driver blew his horn a quarter mile from the house. I ran to the school bus welling up inside with emotion. I ran on board and rushed to my seat. I began to weep uncontrollably. Debora Hayes who was two years older than me came to my side and put her arm around me as everyone stared at us.

She asked me "What's the matter?"

I snubbed saying, "I lost my bird dog."

Our 1957 Ford Fairlane

# How Not to Rattle Up a Buck

The one hundred-acre tract of land that bordered our forty-acre farm was a wooded area owned by Phillip's sister, my great aunt Laura. I often squirrel hunted with my new .22 rifle on that property. The way I stalked for squirrel also presented an unexpected introduction to large game.

As I crept stealthily on a ridge through the woods focusing on a squirrel, in a solitaire meadow below me I saw flashes of white like a flock of egrets flying through the woods. It appeared as if their long wingspan flapped up and down as they flew close to the ground through the meadow and into the woods. With a second glance at this beautiful scene, I realized I was witnessing my first encounter with a large herd of whitetail deer.

1968 was the first year Oconee County, Georgia, had a whitetail deer season. The deer seemed to be plentiful, especially on the additional 120-acre farm the family had purchased a half-mile down the Kirkland Road. There was one big buck that was catching everyone's attention. By today's standards he would score about 140 points for a typical eight-point buck. The reason I am sure of this is founded in a discovery I made a year later when I went for a drive out to our 120-acre farm to scout around.

I was idling along in the old 1957 Ford on the field road when I saw something that looked suspiciously like a deer antler. Its tines were pointing upward out of the tall grass. I stopped and retrieved one shed antler from the buck I had named Big Boy. It scored seventy points and was a massive specimen. I still have that shed after many years. The rack he was proudly displaying by the time I found the shed had to score even higher. So I devised a plan to rattle him in for the kill.

Bobby had graduated and would soon leave for Paducah, Kentucky, for his first job. He too had concerns about the draft but had been previously deferred because of a kidney disorder. I talked him into the plan to bag Big Boy. I had read in the outdoor magazines that bucks would come to the rattling of antlers if it thought other bucks were invading its territory. I needed someone to hide in a blind near where I was hunting and rattle together the smaller antlers I had collected; Big Boy was sure to come running in. Then I would ambush him. Bobby agreed. I strategically positioned Bobby in heavy cover about thirty yards away with the antlers and told him to wait thirty minutes as I silently and slowly moved to where I would hunt. I had purchased a 7.7 Japanese army rifle from a surplus store in Athens for $20. It did not have a sling attached to it, so I had to carry it in my hands while I hunted. The spot from which I had chosen to shoot was a large water oak with many limbs on it. This would make it easier for me to climb up ten or fifteen feet, sit on a larger limb, and wait for the unsuspecting "Big Boy" to rush in.

    I had allowed a thirty-minute window to be as quiet as we could be and get settled for at least fifteen minutes with no movement at all before Bobby was to start the rattling. I was on time with my plan as I started quietly up the large tree with my rifle. I would place the rifle on the limb above me and use both of my hands to climb to that level and repeat the steps until I was about twelve feet off the ground. About half way up, I took the rifle and again reached up to the next big limb when the limb my foot was on gave way with a big crack. Down I crashed, breaking every small- and medium-sized limb my 185-pound body came in contact with. My back impacted the ground, and my rifle, which I was holding in both hands, smacked me across the chest. I struggled to catch the breath that had been knocked from me. Before I could breathe I heard Bobby in the bush begin rattling, "rattle, rattle, rattle," a pause and then, "rattle, rattle, rattle," again and again.

    I realized as I lay there that the hunt was over, but it hurt too much to laugh. I gathered my wits and slowly got to my feet and walked over to where Bobby was incessantly rattling those horns.

I peeked into the dense cover and said, "Bobby! What are you doing?"

Bobby said in an excited way that I seldom see, "Right after you left, something went crashing through the brush. Didn't you hear it?"

Then I laughed. I did not know at that point which one of us was the bigger dummy. I confessed, "Bobby, that noise you heard was me, falling out of the tree."

We both laughed and walked home.

Cheryl Marie Anderson, 1971

# IT CAN'T BE LUCK

Billy Boyd Lavender, 1967

# Girls in School

I began dating a girl named Carol in Maxey's, Georgia, that I had met at a church function. She was an Oglethorpe County cheerleader who lived across the Oconee River. She was a junior as I started my senior year at Oconee High School. Carol and her two sisters were gifted "A" students. Eligible students of the Maxey's community, Carol and her sisters could receive a scholarship from a grant left by an elderly rich woman who had lived there. Carol's immediate future was solid. However, my future was on shifting sand.

There was another girl that attended Antioch that had caught my attention. In fact it was the year before she transferred from the Watkinsville Elementary School into the eighth grade at Oconee High School. I was sitting on the school bus when I first noticed Cheryl Anderson on her way home a few blocks away. The summer of 1966 was fast approaching, and school would soon be out. Some of the younger boys on the bus were teasing one another about their relationship with her as she walked by.

Boisterously they teased, "There goes your woman!"

It was loud enough for Cheryl to look in their direction. She had her arms folded around her books as she walked. Modestly she jerked her head back straight and raised her chin as if to say in a chiding way, "Humph!" It was an expression I have seen and heard from her for the subsequent fifty-one years.

Cheryl's birthday came in January, and she was already a young teenager of thirteen before entering junior high school in 1966. I was sixteen. Both Cheryl and I were developing into physical maturity at an alarming rate. The only difference was I was a foot taller and fifty pounds heavier, but I still could not take my eyes off her. So when the Christian Youth Fellowship at Antioch had their hayride, I asked her to go with me. She accepted my invitation.

Cheryl was a quiet girl, and I had to be particularly attentive to notice if she really liked me. Because I had my driver's license, I dated other girls. Then I met Carol Herring, and she took up most of my courting time in 1967. Though I saw Cheryl at church, I had decided that I was too old for her.

Once I met Carol at choir practice to offer her a ride home afterward. There were no men in the choir, so I sat nearby in the pews and sang along with them. Their choir director heard me and asked me to come over and sit with them. After we had practiced a few more hymns, their choir director asked me directly if I would sing a solo special during their upcoming revival. That type of request had never been made of me before. After the insistence of Carol and the other women, I relented and agreed that I would.

I did not know at that time that Antioch Christian Church was a denominational sister church to Maxey's Christian Church. When the night of my solo came, I was sitting behind the revival preacher as the pews began to fill. At first there were only a few parishioners, and then an influx of Antioch members from my church started arriving in support of the Maxey's revival. As each additional member from my church started to enter, the more nervous I became.

Somehow I made it through the solo, and afterward the Antioch members that had come chimed in with their accolades and insisted that I would now have to sing at our revival.

That night began a ministry in music that has lasted for over a half century. I have sung in worship services and at funerals, weddings, and memorial services not counting my many band performances.

I reluctantly followed the instruction and encouragement of my family. I worked at odd jobs during the summer months of 1967–1969. I worked as a yardman for Mr. Adams, one of Bobby's bosses at The Department of Agriculture. Next I worked at the Puritan Cordage Mill before I was hired for summer help at The Department of Agriculture in 1968 and 1969.

I was accepted for attendance at Truett McConnell College in Cleveland, Georgia, in the fall of 1968 after high school graduation.

Financially it took more than what I had saved from my summer jobs just to attend one quarter. Collectively the family could not afford another quarter of junior college. Bobby suggested that I attend night school at the University of Georgia for one quarter to prove I could do university work and then request a transfer.

It was imperative that I stay in school or I would be drafted. The director of night school and I made an agreement that if I made "As" in both my night courses, he would transfer me into day school as a commuter.

One of my courses was speech, and the other was Accounting 111. I had taken Accounting 110 the quarter before, and I thought I would do well enough to get the transfer. Speech did not present a problem. However, the final test for Accounting 111 was quite peculiar to me. The test was one long problem. To prove his point, the instructor required that there be no mathematical errors. To pass and receive an "A," no errors were allowed. Any errors at all and it meant failure. By that single fact, I failed. It seemed unfair to me, but, nevertheless, my hopes of a college education were dashed.

The pressure I was feeling was near intolerable. The pressure of failing was one thing. The pressure of disappointing my parents and Bobby was also heavy. But the real "elephant in the room" was the draft and the Vietnam War. The days I spent between failing Accounting 111 and registration for the next quarter were miserable. I needed to talk to my parents.

I was unusually quiet as Dad and I rode down Lumpkin Street and by the coliseum in the old pickup. The new coliseum was where Bobby had just graduated with a bachelor's degree in business. It was already past time for my parents and family to know that I had failed at my attempt to get the transfer.

I took a deep breath and was about to speak when Dad spoke proudly, "That's where I want to see you graduate in a few years."

I was crushed. How could I disappoint him with the news I had. I don't know what I thought would happen when they found out, but I put off telling them even longer.

The pressure I was filling became more unbearable. The time came for registration, so Dad gave me two blank signed checks, one for registration and one for books. In my immature and muddled mind, I tried thinking of what I might do that would make the family proud of me instead of the shame I had brought on myself by failing in school. So on a whim, I wrote a detailed letter explaining the pressure I was feeling and how sorry I was for disappointing them and left it under Dad's pillow. I cashed the two checks, filled up the Impala with gasoline, and headed for Nashville.

The Hardigree/Haulbrook House, 1968

Dad and Bossy, 1968

# Facing the Music, a Forlorn Hope

I was truly confused and half out of my mind. I remember crossing the state line into Tennessee about 2:00 p.m. I had hoped to get to Nashville by sundown. I arrived in Murfreesboro, Tennessee, during the rush hour, and the traffic was really horrible, but by the time I reached Nashville it was even worse as the sun was setting. I was feeling very alone and sad and decided to forgo a shot at a recording contract and continued on past Nashville and decided if I could talk to Bobby, everything would be OK. So I headed north to Chicago where Bobby had taken a job with City Service Oil Corp. I had completely avoided my Invisible Friend while I was feeling this pressure, but he appointed a guardian angel to watch over me.

I bought a bottle of No Doz and put my knowledge of geography to work. It was a strange night trip alone. I drove north through one city after another taking all the main highways north with the radio blasting. The first time I saw Chicago on a sign, it read 150 miles. I pressed onward and northward in the pitch darkness. Each time I filled up the car, I noticed that the dialect of the service station attendants had changed from the southern drawl to northern Yankee.

It was about 7:00 a.m. when I arrived in the suburbs of Chicago. I filled up with gas one more time and asked the attendant if he knew where the apartments that Bobby lived in were located. He did not. After the second or third stop, I discovered I was on the south side of Chicago and the apartments were on the west side. I continued to ask directions until I saw the apartments in the distance. I remember entering the building on the bottom floor where the mailboxes were located. I was able to get an apartment number from there with Bobby's name on it.

Bobby had a male roommate, and he came to the door when I knocked. I put my finger over my lips and said, "Shhhhh. Where is Bobby?" I don't remember if I told him I was Bobby's brother or if he figured it out, but he let me in. I tiptoed down the hallway and cracked open the door. Bobby had the cover pulled up around his neck, but his eyes were wide open, listening for who it was at the door. He was totally surprised when I landed on top of him. I was so happy to see him. He had a lot of questions, but I had the answers. Before he ever rose from the side of his bed, I remember him saying, "You came in on a wing and a prayer."

Bobby was so kind and understanding, but the first thing he did was to call Mom and Dad to let them know I was safe. They too were understanding and told me to take a few days before returning home. That evening Bobby had his new girlfriend, Linda, to come over for a little party they threw for the weekend. His roommate had his girlfriend over too. Though we did not know it at the time, Bobby and Linda would later wed, and she would become part of our family.

We had a grand few days together, but inevitably I had to move on toward home. Bobby took me to see *Bullet*, a Steve McQueen movie. I remember when we left the movie theater in Chicago. The wind was brutal as it blew off the frigid waters of the Great Lakes. Bobby pulled his overcoat close and shuddered, "The 'hawk' is out tonight!" It put a cold and lonely shudder in my bones also. Somehow I was beginning to realize things would never be the same between us, as our lives would go in separate directions from that time forward.

Bobby had worked in Paducah, Kentucky, for a while before taking the position with City Service Oil Corp. He called some close friends in Paducah and asked them if they would put me up for the night when I came through. These folks had a daughter my age, and Bobby hinted that I might take her out. I took his advice on both recommendations. I would not feel so pushed on my trip back home.

I had not given my Invisible Friend the proper acknowledgment that he so deserved during my latter teen years. Nevertheless, he was with me.

I had breakfast with the host family in Paducah and thanked them for their hospitality and headed home. By noon I was getting sleepy as I wound my way through the mountains of Paducah, Kentucky. The tremendous pressure I was feeling on the trip up was subsiding somewhat. However, a decision had to be made concerning my immediate future.

A shower of rain had wet the pavement as I approached a sharp curve in the road ahead. The route had been blasted through solid rock on both sides. It was a narrow passage, and I was going much too fast. I tried to follow the lines in the road, but the rear end of the Impala broke loose, and I was out of control. As I fought to regain control, the solid rock, my Invisible Friend, caught the right rear bumper ever so slightly and set me straight in the road. He was speaking to me, and I heard him loud and clear. I thanked him. Then I reflected back on what Bobby had said, "You came in on a wing and a prayer." I had experienced one of several miracles in my life, and it was all because of the abiding presence of my Invisible Friend.

I still had some money in my savings account that I had put aside for books and registration had my transfer to the University of Georgia been successful. After arriving back home, it was clear Mom and Dad had accepted the fact that I would not be finishing college.

Dad said, "Your heart just wasn't in it."

I was still feeling guilty about hoodwinking my parents and surprised Mom with a new refrigerator. I paid cash for it and had it delivered.

For the spring of 1969, I helped Dad on the farm and would have been satisfied to do only that for the foreseeable future. But I was not surprised when I received the expected draft notice. My choices had become crystal clear. It was the Air Force, Navy, or Vietnam.

The day I went to the recruiting office, the Air Force recruiter wasn't in a good mood as I heard him in a confrontation with a subordinate. Through the next door down the Navy recruiter stood smiling with an extended hand. That was all it took to draw me into his office.

Recruiters are skilled at what they do. They can make serving Uncle Sam sound mighty grand to an impressionable young man.

They heavily accentuate the positive aspects and leave the rest for the drill instructors. I signed up to become a sailor. I would remain a civilian until August of 1969. The pressure I had been experiencing for several years was gone. Suddenly, I felt freer even though I had obligated myself to the Navy.

Cheryl and I were together at several church functions at the Antioch hayrides, volleyball, and softball games. We only double dated twice when she was still fifteen. Once she was allowed to go to the Atlanta Braves game with her older first cousin, Mary Lou, and her boyfriend, Bobby Bishop, and me. We had a good time. The other time I double dated with her was with her best friend Beth and my good friend Edwin. Cheryl was sixteen, and I was eighteen. I soon would have a birthday in the summer of 1969. At this age falling in love was a hit or miss proposition. It was sort of like making a profession of faith. Sometimes you say "I love you" not knowing what you are getting into. On this double date in the summer of 1969, I told Cheryl I loved her. I did not want her to feel she had to say anything back to me when I said it to her. I should not have concerned myself about that, because she didn't.

To this day I still don't know when Cheryl fell in love with me. We still laugh about that, and she has kept that secret for herself. We agreed to write each other when I left for nine weeks of basic training. We would remain faithful to each other and write to one another. It was a one-sided agreement since I would be locked down with all boys. Cheryl on the other hand had two more years of school. She was becoming more beautiful every year, and the boys were noticing her. She had two kinds of beauty. One beauty was on the surface, and the other was the one that ran deep. She had both, and I cherished her. We kept our promises to each other in 1969.

# Basic Training

Prior to 1969, the Navy had only two basic training facilities in America. One was in San Diego, California, and the other was in Michigan. I would be sent to the new facility in Orlando, Florida.

My folks took me to Atlanta for my induction and swearing in. All the civilian recruits were lined up and given a general overall impromptu health inspection. We were then given a cot to sleep on and one last evening of civilian life before reporting back at 7:00 a.m. sharp for the roll call.

The next day we were bussed to Orlando, Florida, through the late evening and night hours. All of us were sleep deprived when we arrived on base early the next morning. I don't remember breakfast, but I'm sure we had something. The first main order of business was testing. I remember we were still in our civilian clothes. My two elder brothers had told me that this part of the process was very important and had impressed upon me to do my very best no matter what the circumstances were.

That gave me an edge. I could see boys with their heads down snoring. I was determined to ace the test if it were possible to do so. It was a difficult period for mental concentration, but I did my best. It was reflected in my scores that came out at the end of the nine weeks.

We were then bussed to the uniform facilities building. I can still smell the blue denim dye that permeated that place. We were literally measured up and down and around from head to toe and systematically channeled in the direction to receive our sea bag inventory. Everything we would ever need for wherever we might be sent was in that bag.

We were bussed to a location just outside the barracks we would be assigned to live in for the next nine weeks. Before we off-loaded,

Chief Bistadue stepped onto the bus and made his introduction. He informed us that we would become Drill Company 164. None of us knew what that meant, but we found out later. Being in a drill company had a proud distinction from the other companies training with us at the same time. We would be a performance group providing a "pass and review" inspection for the top brass for as many as four graduations. That meant we would be trained to performance level at six weeks and perform at three graduations before performing at our own.

The drill company had three sections. It has the Main Flag Corp., comprised of most of the company's recruits, and it also had a drill team of twenty-four. Within the twenty-four members on the drill team, twelve of them were the honor guard.

Chief Bistadue made his initial introduction to the busload of recruits and then stood right outside the opened bi-folded doors of the bus. He began picking twenty-four candidates for the drill team. He made twenty-four of us form a single file line and began shouting drill commands to each recruit one at a time.

"Right face!" "Left face!" "About face!"

I could see out of the corner of my eye what he was trying to get them to do. By the time he got to me, I put it all to good use.

After he saw my effort to follow his commands, he commented. "I think we can dress you up." He had selected me from the twenty-four drill team members to be one of the twelve on the honor guard. We had not spent a full twenty-four hours in basic training, and I had no idea as to what all of that meant. However, we were about to learn.

One of the recruits had been a drill team captain in high school. He was appointed that job for our company's drill team. He was an excellent captain.

In addition to the normal basic training that all recruits received, the drill company also had to put in two hours of drill practice for precision performances every day. Often, these two hours were unsupervised by instructors. Our drill company captain was the only authority figure during this time. He taught us some pretty cool maneuvers from his high school drill team. Since I was a singer I was appointed to be the cadence caller for the entire company, except for those two hours. The extra drill time that we put in to be ready in six weeks made our company the envy of the entire base. I made sure everyone knew we were coming, and the rest of the company responded with the sound of their boots. I must say we were something to hear and to see. Chief Bistadue told us that only one other company had even come close to our excellence. During the last week of training, he rewarded us by getting approval for one day of liberty off base and bought 3 percent draft beer for the entire company.

The usual basic naval training includes personal hygiene, naval terminology, drill, naval history, inspections, discipline, and physical fitness. A mop became a swab. A hat became a cover. The right side of anything was starboard. The left side of anything was port. The restroom became the head, etc., and we ran or marched everywhere we needed to go on the base.

All recruits for the first four weeks wore blue denim shirts and bell-bottom dungarees with a blue ball cap or cover. The normal white covers all sailors wear were only issued in the fifth week. By then the numerous washings our denim had received began to fade it to a lighter blue. When we combined our white covers with the lighter blue faded denim, we were called "salty," a distinction of seniority.

Mail call was the highlight of the day for all of us. It was disappointing not to receive a letter for even one day, but Cheryl was faithful to keep them coming and so were my parents.

Behind the scenes our basic battery scores were being evaluated by the Navy personnel department. The scores determined what a recruit was best suited for, and the personnel department would draft orders to send them to their next command. Receiving any kind of "A" school was preferable to becoming an undesignated apprentice and being sent anywhere in the navy including a ship. A recruit's pay grade is E-1. After basic training almost everyone's pay grade is E-2, seaman apprentice. A week or two before we finished basic training, we received our orders according to our basic battery scores, and some recruits became "designated strikers."

The cutoff score for Radioman "A" School was a combined general, clerical, technical, and arithmetic score of 106. I scored 106 and was sent to become a "designated striker" at the Radioman "A" School in Bainbridge, Maryland. Being a striker meant four things. We were permitted to sew on the patch that designated the specific field we were attempting to work in. Second, we were exempted from work details or "working parties" that were comprised of lower-ranking enlisted personnel. Third, we were needed in message centers on base and radio central aboard ships to communicate for Uncle Sam twenty-four hours a day. Fourth, we were background investigated for a minimum clearance level of secret.

The school was six months long. I graduated from Radioman "A" School as an E-3 Radioman Seaman in the spring of 1970. It was the beginning of a forty-five-year career in what is now called information technology.

It was sometime later before I saw the complete results of my basic battery scores. In all the fields where the Navy needed personnel, my scores ranged from 103 to 123.

In all the branches of military service, physical fitness is paramount. Running ensured that a recruit was fit for service at the end of his training. As a rule, if only three or more recruits needed to go anywhere on the base, we formed a "detail" and marched to that location. If an errand required only one recruit, it meant you ran.

Little qualification was needed to perform the various duties of running a company of recruits during basic training. When our company commander discovered my mother had worked at Snow White Laundry, I was appointed laundry PO. For nine weeks I pushed a dolly loaded with the companies' dirty laundry to the base laundry. Immediately after drop-off I ran back to my barracks and joined my company. This meant that every laundry day, I ran to and from the base laundry twice. In that era salt tablets were available at all the water fountains on base. It was very important to stay hydrated during the summer months at the Orlando facility. Recruits were expected to take a salt tablet every time they drank water. Often it was too much, and the excessive salt would sweat out through the pores of the skin and collect there.

I was six feet tall and weighed 185 pounds when I went to Orlando. After basic training I weighed 165 pounds, and my appearance was almost frail. I had two weeks leave before I had to report to Bainbridge, Maryland. Mom's home cooking quickly restored me to my optimum weight.

Cheryl and I discovered our desire to be with each other more and more during the two weeks before my "A" school. It was a very special time for our relationship. The old nemesis of pressure started to creep in as I became concerned about leaving Cheryl behind so often and moving around the country and soon to be world. She was finishing her junior year of high school and would start her senior year in the fall of 1970. I did not know it at the time, but by the fall of 1970, I would be stationed halfway around the world.

# Radioman "A" School

The winter of 1969–1970 in Maryland was brutal. It was quite a contrast from the weather I had experienced in Orlando, Florida. The heavy wool peacoat that had been issued to us was put to good use in Bainbridge. It was not uncommon to march in the snow that stayed on the ground a week at a time. The wind would cut through our denim dungarees and bite the skin. It was fortunate that all the facilities on the base were in close proximity to each other and exposure to the elements was limited.

Cheryl and I wrote to each other frequently, but the six months of school seemed like an eternity as compared to the first nine weeks away from home. Increasingly I was feeling concerned that our relationship would suffer from being apart so much of the time.

For 1969–1970, the radioman class at Bainbridge, Maryland, was intense and demanding. The training for communications had evolved from the knowledge and experiences of our naval predecessors since World War I. We were taught Morse code telegraph, voice radio procedure, the military phonetic alphabet, and the state-of-the-art teletype using ship to shore procedure, ship to ship, message handling, security classifications, precedence, and message format. We learned the nomenclature of all the related transmitters, receivers, and their frequency ranges. We learned about propagation and the correct equipment to use with the proper frequency.

We were taught telegraph using Morse code at the beginning of our training. We used headphones with prerecorded speeds starting with a slow five words per minute. On our first day the instructor let us hear what Morse code sounded like in the first week and what we would be listening to at the end of the training. We were doubtful we would ever learn to decipher such a fast stream of dots and dashes.

For the first few weeks of school, classmates would talk to each other in Morse code using the phonetic alphabet. "A" was alpha, dit-dah, etc. It helped in learning the process. We not only learned to receive it but transmit it also. After a week we were introduced to the hand key. CW stands for communication wave, a constant tone that was broken by the hand key into dots and dashes for characters and words, so the timing and space between them had to maintain a consistent rhythm. By the end of the first month of school I could send sixteen words a minute and receive thirty-five words a minute with less than five errors.

Before the class moved on to other phases of becoming a radioman, the instructor that had been teaching telegraph made a historical announcement. He said, "This 1970 class is the last class at the Navy Radioman "A" School that will ever be taught Morse code, CW, and the telegraph."

The historical significance was the importance that Morse code had been as a primary means of communicating in America since the last days of the "Pony Express." It was just the beginning, however, of rapid and monumental changes in information technology for the next half-century. I would make it a career after my discharge from the military and discover that it would require me to be schooled in the many new methods of modern communication.

About midway through the six-month school, we were introduced to the teletype. I had taken typing in high school and was fairly proficient, typing about forty words per minute. The only similarities between typewriters and the electronic teletype were the keyboard. On the teletype, with the slightest touch, a proficient operator could type upward of sixty words per minute.

Radioman "A" School, 1970, Bainbridge, Maryland

# Breaking the Heart of an Angel

The last part of Radioman "A" School was in a secure location, and all personnel leaving or entering wore yellow identification badges on a chain around their necks. This area was known as "Prac Deck." I never understood if it meant practice deck or practical deck or both. Students for the first time could see the similarities of message centers at shore stations and radio centrals aboard ship. Few American citizens in or out of the military are permitted into these areas. It was a strange and complicated environment in which to work and study. Nothing was taken into or from the Prac Deck. Talking about the inside of Prac Deck was prohibited outside the area. A golden rule taught to all strikers to help clarify the different levels of clearances was a question they must ask themselves. "Does the person I am talking to have *a need to know?*" Honestly answering that question eliminated a vast majority of all cleared personnel up to the highest levels. Clearances do not necessarily allow ranking commissioned officers to enter secure spaces or discuss message content.

It was during this phase of training the class was given an opportunity to put in a request for orders. It did not mean you would get your request approved, but if personnel were needed in the location you requested, it could happen. One of the choices offered was brother duty. My eldest brother, Roger, had just been ordered to a submarine tender in the trust territory of Guam. What I would be requesting was called preferred sea duty. That's what I requested, and I received orders to the new Naval Communications Station, Guam.

As the orders I received continued to separate me miles and miles further from home, I feared my relationship with Cheryl would also widen. So in an awkward attempt to free her from our private obligations, I wrote her a letter and mailed it without talking it over with my Invisible Friend.

I was never more miserable from the time I mailed that letter than I was through the sleepless nights ahead into the next day and into the week ahead. My Invisible Friend effectively took me to the woodshed, and the peace I had known had left me. The nights were filled with nightmares. I tossed and turned through the nights with visions of the first time I had ever noticed Cheryl. There were echoing haunts of "There goes your woman!" and then childish laughter afterward. I had visions of approaching Cheryl to apologize and she would turn away as if to say, "Humph!"

I had become aware that I was truly in love with Cheryl Anderson, but it was too late. I had already mailed the letter, and she surely must have received it since four days had gone by. The only thing that I knew to do was to make a long distance call home to Cheryl and spill my guts to her. I asked her if she had received that horrible letter.

Trying not to show her emotion, she answered, "Yes. Have you received mine?"

I sadly said, "No."

She said I would be receiving it soon.

We both agreed to ignore the contents of each of our letters, but I read hers anyway.

How could I have been so stupid? I had broken the heart of an angel. I'm no forensic scientist, but I could have sworn that the ink in the words I read was smeared from her teardrops. If the misery I had put her through was just half of what I had experienced, I deserved every bit of the discipline my Invisible Friend was applying to me. Both of our hearts would mend initially with more loving letter correspondence, but not until we could touch and hug one another would everything finally be OK.

The time came in the spring of 1970 when I graduated from Radioman "A" School. I took two weeks leave at home before flying to Guam. The relationship between Cheryl and I grew closer than ever. We spent every available moment together. She still had her senior year to finish high school, and we knew that had to come first.

But I wanted her to know I had more serious plans for our future. To show her, I gave her a preengagement diamond teardrop necklace before I left. We began to talk about marriage around the obligations of her school and my obligations with the Navy. I would not return home from Guam until October of 1971. We both agreed we would marry then.

# Nimitz Hill Message Center, Guam

The flight to Guam took thirteen hours over the Western Pacific Ocean. Most of the passengers were military personnel with their dependents. There was nothing to see but water below us. When we arrived at Andersen Air Force Base, we off-loaded down a ramp and received our sea bag and luggage from the underside of the huge jet. My first step onto the solid ground was a learning experience. My new slick and shiny black dress shoes slipped on the coral-paved tarmac. I fell. Coral is used like gravel to pave everything on Guam. It is as slick as ice especially after becoming wet. I took that as an omen to drive and tread the pavement carefully for the next eighteen months.

I was very fortunate to have loved ones already established and living in Navy housing on the naval base when I arrived. All I had to do was contact them and let them know I had arrived, and I immediately had a personal chauffeur. They provided all the transportation I needed for my first day on Guam.

A general explanation about the geography of Guam can be summed up in a few statements. Guam is the largest of the Marianas Islands. It is thirty miles long and eight miles wide. Beautiful coral reefs and a few nice beaches surround it. It is mountainous in the center. The U.S. military personnel make up over 50 percent of its population, and the rest are of native Guamanian decent.

A trust territory is vital to the strategic interest of the United States. Likewise it was critical to the Japanese Empire in World War II. The Japanese occupied it for three years after the first battle of Guam in 1941. Ironically Radioman George Ray Tweed was the only American not captured after the first battle. The native islanders kept him under cover as he signaled in Morse code the positions of Japanese forces to the U.S. Navy ships from the mouth of his cave.

## IT CAN'T BE LUCK

The American forces reoccupied Guam in 1944 after the second battle of Guam.

As a young history buff, I discovered that the large bomb craters left in the coral reefs were not only interesting to snorkel over but found them very beautiful. It was simply awesome to witness the panoramic view of the many schools of fish dashing and darting in the underwater pool. The reflection of colors, off the white sands of the bomb crater that had drifted thirty feet down, was breathtaking.

On the opposite ends of the island were the naval station and Andersen Air Force Bases. In the middle was the Naval Communications Station, Guam. One main highway connects the three military bases. A few miles from the naval base was the gated area of the USS *Proteus*, the submarine tender where Roger worked. Across the main highway and up Nimitz Hill was the administrative building where Admiral Pugh's headquarters was located. Admiral Pugh was the commander of the naval forces in the Marinas Islands. A few miles down the main highway from the Andersen Air Force Base was the Naval Communications Station. That location housed the Navy's communication personnel until their clearances became final and were dispatched for duty in various facilities across the island.

It became obvious right away that I needed a means of transportation to better facilitate my eighteen months of brother duty and my visitations with the family. The good morale of the unmarried enlisted personnel was enhanced greatly by the Enlisted Men's Clubs on all the bases. Likewise the Commissioned Officers Clubs were provided on a grand scale. On the other hand all married personnel and their families considered Guam as good duty.

Shortly after arriving at the Communication Station, I asked Roger to take me to a motorcycle shop so I could look over the new bikes. I purchased a Honda 50 cc motorbike. I practiced off-road maneuvers until I could operate it well enough to pass the test required to obtain a license.

I was successful in obtaining the license and was then free to travel anywhere on the island. I obtained a base sticker, which allowed me to enter and leave any base on Guam. The freedom the bike afforded me was a tremendous asset and made brother duty more fun and the stay at my first duty station much more tolerable.

Most of the personnel at the Communication Station were young E-2 and E-3 designated strikers. The rest were noncommissioned petty officers and commissioned officers in the administrative and leadership positions. Before these strikers were dispatched to work professionally in their designated fields, a background investigation was conducted on each one. This background investigation began at the beginning of "A" school. This investigation was done behind the scenes and unbeknownst to the striker. Often, to obtain the proper clearance for where a striker would work, it took up to six months to complete. Some clearances were secret and others were top secret. Until these final background investigations were completed, the daily routine for these strikers was similar to an extension of basic training. Brass needed polishing. Decks needed swabbing. Uniforms needed laundering. Berthing areas needed field days. The mess hall needed workers to assist the excellent Guamanian cooks, etc.

The chow at the Naval Communications Station was excellent. While working in the scullery, washing the dishes and silverware, I had the opportunity to become more acquainted with the cooks. Every week, while I waited on my final clearance, somewhere on the island a huge fiesta was held. All the boys working in the mess hall for that week were invited to the grand party. One such fiesta, the first I attended, I will never forget. It was right on the main strip that connected all the bases. I rode my bike there and anticipated a great time of food fellowship and fun.

The food was displayed in a buffet style setting, and it was beautifully arranged. As I piled the food onto my plate, I was particularly interested in a large bowl of chicken salad and generously added it to my selections. The first bite of food I put in my mouth was the chicken salad. It was delicious, but I did not know I was supposed to work my way up to it. My eyes began to water, my nose ran, and sweat popped out under my eyes and on top of my head. It was my first introduction to their Habanero peppers. Before I could take another bite, I was desperately looking for something to drink to put out the fire. Though it is certainly not advisable to drink and drive a motorcycle, at that moment, I was not concerned about that. To my relief, nearby was a tub of ice filled to the brim with beer. So long as I was swallowing something cold, I could breath. After two or three beers in as many minutes, the pain began to subside. My new Guamanian friends thought it was hilarious, and soon we all settled into a wonderful meal of Guamanian-style, grilled chicken, pork ribs, and all the trimmings.

Guam 1971

Guam 1971

# The Antagonist

On Guam working in the scullery in June of 1970, the conditions were less than desirable. The temperature often reached above 120 degrees from the steam generated by cleaning the dishes and silverware. The boys working there would literally be drenched with sweat and steam, and we often had to take breaks just to cool off and get a breath of fresh air. This particular evening I was finding it difficult to catch my breath, and it wasn't caused from eating peppers. I tried catching my breath on the steps in front of the mess hall. I knew I was taking a long break, and I either needed to go back to work or get help. The dispensary was next door with personnel on duty. I went there and was checked in by an E-6 hospital corpsman. He listened to my heart with his stethoscope and took my blood pressure. To say the least, he was alarmed and called his superior. I heard him say to the doctor, "His heartbeat is irregular, his pulse rate is a shallow at 120, and his blood pressure is 180/110." There was a pause as he listened to his instructions. Within minutes I was put on a gurney and placed in an ambulance, and away we sped to the Naval Hospital Guam with the siren wailing. The excitement of it all was not helping as I desperately tried to get some answers from the corpsman attending me. They had no answers.

It had been exactly ten years from the time Mrs. Marsh, the county nurse, had noticed the irregularity in my heart rhythm when I was ten years old. Silently I asked myself the question, "Could this be the same old nemesis?"

The first of what was to be many electrocardiograph tests was taken of my heart that day. The results were inconclusive. The doctor that read the EKG showed me on the graph a slight blip in my heart rhythm. It was the first indicator of an abnormality with my heart;

however, it was not considered to be a serious condition. Medical technology had not advanced enough at that time to know what the long-term ramifications might be. At the time it was a very deep and shady area of cardiac electrophysiology. All the doctor could do on this day was to put me on Librium, a tranquilizer, and prescribe a week of light duty.

Once my heart reverted back to its normal rhythm, it did not take me long to realize the pills were incapacitating me to the extreme. I could hardly function, and I feared I might be disciplined for lack of performance. At my follow-up appointment, I told the doctor how "smashed" the tranquilizers made me feel. He asked how I was doing otherwise, and I told him I felt better without them. He instructed me to flush them down the toilet, and I did. That was the end of that episode from the "antagonist."

# IT CAN'T BE LUCK

Cheryl's Fun in '71'

Cheryl's Fun in "71"

# Letters from Home

My daily assignments on the Naval Communications Station were becoming mundane. As in basic training, receiving letters from home was the most cherished part of the day. The Enlisted Men's Club, liberty to snorkel the reefs, and touring the island helped, but even a large island like Guam becomes small after a few weeks. I became the lead singer and rhythm guitarist in another band. The most senior member of the band was a chief corpsman. We practiced at his house and received multiple offers to play at the chief's club.

Some of the letters I was receiving from home indicated that the FBI had sent agents in black suits to my neighborhood in the country to inquire about my past. The neighbors that were interviewed obviously told my parents. Apparently all went well at these neighborhood interviews. The end result was a top secret clearance for me. The duty station to which I would be permanently assigned for the rest of my tour had several names. One title was top of the Mar.; another was com. Nav. Mar., short for commander of Naval Forces, Marianas Islands. Working in Admiral Pugh's office or in the Nimitz Hill Message Center was all the same location.

Working in Admiral Pugh's message center meant several things. The entire group of "designated strikers" that were cleared for that level was kept together for accountability reasons. After all, "loose lips sink ships." We were transferred to the opposite end of the island to the naval station where my brother and his family were living. One whole barracks was assigned to the Nimitz Hill Message Center personnel. As a result, a close bond between shipmates was developed. There was never a more diverse group of young men put together to live in the same space. We all seemed to "have each other's back," in a professional way, but individually we were as different as the ethnicity in the American citizenship. Also working in Admiral Pugh's office meant you worked for President Nixon's brother-in-law.

Once I had arrived at the naval station where my brother and family were living, I visited with them more often. Since Cheryl and I had discussed our marriage arrangements for October of 1971, it was incumbent upon me to provide that, ever so important, engagement ring. The jewelry counter at the Guam Navy Exchange did not have an extensive selection. It did, however, have a range of quality diamonds.

On one end was the most expensive diamond. As I gazed down the length of the counter, it became obvious the quality of the jewelry diminished in value and quality. I visited this counter several times before making a selection. The most expensive solitaire engagement ring was the very first one on display. It glittered and danced in the light just like an animal in a pet store reaching out as if to say, "Pick me!" It seemed expensive so I delayed my purchase.

I started to put away some of my pay to be able to purchase Cheryl's engagement ring. Financially, I scraped every way I could. I even took the allotment I was given for food and put it away. My sister-in-law, Sonia, noticed I was losing weight. I lost from 185 pounds down to 175, and I looked frail to her. She started having me over for supper and lunch in an effort to put the weight back on before October. By May 1971 Cheryl's senior year in high school was almost finished. I was six foot even and weighed 195 pounds.

Back home Cheryl was developing into a beautiful young woman. I did not have the advantage of noticing that development since I was stationed halfway around the world. Nevertheless, Cheryl remained faithful to me and wrote regularly. There was never any trouble between us, but the attention she was receiving caused me some concern. She was the FFA Sweetheart, The Homecoming Queen, and selected as a Senior Superlative most likely to succeed. These events meant she needed a beau to accompany her, especially for Homecoming Queen.

I made a decision to purchase the first diamond ring in the counter and sent it home as a special delivery. It was the best that the Navy Exchange had to offer. However, it was as good as any diamond could be. It was rated gem quality, flawless under ten-power magnification, just like Cheryl. Though I wish I could have seen her when she opened the package, I heard plenty from her later about my brash decision to send the diamond as her eighteenth birthday present in January. She later said she could have skinned me alive.

I think it was a good decision because by her own admission she was having a "good ole time." I thought, too good of a time, and I had heard "all is fair in love and war." The night was fast approaching for the Homecoming Queen Ball. Faithfully Cheryl placed the ring upon her finger to the chagrin of every guy that had ever thought they had a chance at derailing our relationship.

Sweetly she wrote me a letter and explained how important it was for her to have a beau for the big event. She gave me the option to choose who should accompany her. Among the ones she offered for my approval was Edwin Bowden. He was a close friend, confidant, and already a war veteran from Vietnam. Reluctantly I relented, but it tore me up inside. I was miserable. It was imperative that I work toward removing this spiritual torture in the middle of my chest. I had been away from Cheryl for a full year, and at this point another six months seemed like a lifetime.

# The Latter Days of May 1971

Against Roger and Sonia's advice, I put in for two weeks leave. They did not want me flying halfway around the world on military aircraft on so little time. They were fearful I would not make it back on time and be *"AWOL" (absent without leave)*. They also were concerned I would mess up the big October wedding. They were certainly making a lot of sense, but let's face it, I was in love, and love is blind and deaf too.

Dozens of military aircraft were flying in and out of Andersen Air Force Base on a daily basis. MAC flights, as they were called, were going in all different directions. Active duty enlisted personnel had the benefit of catching a ride on these MAC flights. My leave began on May 25. I combined my fourteen-day leave period with the eighty hours of liberty that I received after each series of six, eight-hour watch periods. We called our four-section duty 2-2-2 and 80. Connecting the eighty-hours of liberty that came at the beginning and the end of my leave period gave me eight days of additional margin. Another added feature to my plan was a change in policy established to assist servicemen from unintentionally becoming AWOL. That rule was to check in off a leave period at the nearest military facility. Then the serviceman could use his scheduled liberty to arrive back at his duty station. This extended my leave and liberty time to twenty-two days.

On May 22, 1971, three days before my leave began, I arrived at Andersen Air Force Base in my dress blue uniform with a couple of paychecks in my hand. I caught the next flight stateside. That MAC flight had an estimated time of arrival in San Francisco on May 23 at 1300 hours. The flight was not designed for comfort, but the Navy Air Dales were very nice, understanding, and accommodating. When they saw how happy I was to be visiting my fiancée, they enjoyed the romantic *air* even more.

When we stopped only for refueling in Hawaii, I never left the MAC terminal and kept my eye on the aircraft. We were up and away in short order. The soonest and next available MAC flight from San Francisco eastward was to Texas. I took it and paid a taxi to take me to Dallas/Fort Worth Regional Airport. From there I flew as a military standby on Delta Airlines to Atlanta for $60. Flying east into the sun on modern jets causes later ETAs. When I arrived in Atlanta late in the morning on May 24, 1971, I still had my dress blue wool uniform on. It was hot and my skin was sticky.

School days for seniors in high school were cut short if all their credits were finished. Cheryl was home when I called. She was doubly surprised to hear my voice and to hear me say, "I am at the Atlanta airport!" I said, "Come get me!"

She was stunned but made sure I understood that she would have to find Larry, her brother, and arrange the trip.

I said, "I can wait." So I settled into what I expected to be a long rest.

It was time to change into some cooler civilian clothing, so I went to the restroom to change. I had brought with me a thin gray knit shirt and a pair of black dungarees. I folded and stuffed my dress blue uniform back into the duffle bag. My garb was embarrassingly wrinkled, but it felt much better. Nestling down in a comfortable chair in the atrium, I must have fallen asleep and then woke up.

When I stood up to stretch, I heard Cheryl's shrill voice. "Billy! Billy! Billy!"

I was looking everywhere to try to locate that beautiful voice. She was somewhere close by beneath the scurrying air travelers. Louder she screamed. "Billy! Billy! Billy!"

At that moment I turned to the nearest sound and out popped my five foot, one inch, beautiful princess. She hit me with a "full force hug" with her feet barely touching the floor. I will never, as long as I live, ever forget what that hug felt like to the boy who had spent twelve months away from her care and affection. During those few seconds, I was made aware of all that I had missed over the past year. In a low whisper and under my breath, I began to repeat over and over again, "There's no way." It was said in such a way, I did not know if it was the beginning of a statement or the answer to a question that had not been asked or both. This strange utterance continued on until we were leaving the airport.

With our eyes fixed on one another, and sitting very close to each other in the back seat of Larry's car, Cheryl asked. "Why do you keep saying, there's no way?"

Releasing the torture in my chest, I answered back. "There's no way we are waiting for October to get married."

She too took little convincing. It was settled.

With three weeks in front of us, we set about making it happen. There were some preparations I could do myself, but other preparations required both of us. For our parents, it took getting used to the idea. However, they ceased to think about our plans for an October wedding. The first item of business was a blood test. That would take some time. The actual day of the wedding had not been set.

The senior class of 1971 began practicing for their graduation during the last few days of May. The graduation date was June 1, 1971. Mother allowed me to use the Impala the last few days of May while she continued to work at Gallant Belk in downtown Athens. I picked up Cheryl from graduation rehearsal every day. Mother and I spent quality time riding to and from Gallant Belk during this time. Mother wanted wedding pictures and would pay for a photographer. She also wanted me to shine. By that she meant to buy me a new tweed suit and new shoes. The second order of business was being tailored and fitted at the men's store.

Setting the date came last since so much preparation needed to take place first. On May 31, thinking our preparations was done and before Cheryl's last rehearsal, Dad and I talked about the wedding day. My dad seemed to delight in helping me think it through. In some ways it must have reminded him of his wedding day thirty-five years prior. As we dug deeper into the scenario, my answers to his questions seemed satisfactory to him. Then came his bombshell idea. "Why don't you marry right after the graduation?" Then our wheels began to turn rapidly as we bounced one idea after another off each other.

Our church pastor was giving the benediction so he could wed us. Cheryl's bridesmaid, Joan Reese, would graduate with her. We would make an announcement immediately after the benediction so anyone wanting to stay for the wedding ceremony could do so. Cheryl's white dress was mandatory beneath her white graduation gown. She would march out with her diploma, shed the gown, and then march back in with our marriage license to the music of "Here Comes the Bride." No invitations through the mail would be necessary, and all the flowers were in place. All we needed to do was to respectfully notify the appropriate people and make it happen. Cheryl was an appropriate person. At this point my dad and I were the only ones privy to this date. I was pumped! I had more arrangements to make! We had to speak to the high school principal, Mr. McMullen, affectionately called Mr. Mac.

I arrived at Oconee High School as the senior class formed its processional into the gym for the last rehearsal. My heart was overflowing with joy. Cheryl's classmates grinned and chuckled as they saw me approaching the line. They immediately knew something was in the wind. As I reached for Cheryl's hand, I looked her in the eye, and in front of everyone I asked her. "Will you marry me tomorrow night after the graduation?"

She asked. "Can we?"

Then like with Dad, we bounced all the ideas that came flooding in off each other.

She asked. "What about the blood test?"

My answer to that was to first ask the school principal, Mr. Mac, if it met with his approval. Then we would contact our pastor. Then we both would go to Athens to pick up the blood test and then go by to see Mrs. Hammond, the probate judge for our marriage license. Her head was in a spin, but she agreed.

Right on cue, Mr. Mac walked by the processional line. We stopped him and proposed the idea to him. He was a jewel of a man and, with his broad grin, thought it would be a grand idea. We were off to a good start. We then went to the parsonage to talk to Ed

## IT CAN'T BE LUCK

Reese, our pastor. He had known us since we were adolescents. His joy for us also showed through his smiling face with chuckles, and he too was in agreement. About 1:00 p.m. on May 31, 1971, Cheryl and I drove to Athens to get the results of our blood test.

By midafternoon we were at Mrs. Hammond's office in Watkinsville. Cheryl and I were becoming more and more excited about our big day. By this time we had run through the scenario several times and excitedly told Mrs. Hammond about our plans. She was delighted for us; however, she informed us, "Marriage licenses need to be posted for the public to see for three days." Our hearts sank. The disappointment was written all over our faces. Then remarkably, she reached for the blood test results in my hand and said, "But I can fix that!" We stood in silence as she typed for a few minutes and then handed us our license postdated May 29, 1971. What a day May 31 had been for us.

Mike's Fastback Ford

# IT CAN'T BE LUCK

June 1, 1971

# June 1, 1971

The surprises were not over for us. On June 1, the absolute last day for the class of 1971, Cheryl's classmates threw a wedding shower for us in the classroom of the Future Homemakers of America. How special was that? It was awesome! Lavished upon us were all the many wonderful gifts a newlywed couple would need.

Evening was approaching, and I still did not have a "best man." Of course the best man had to be Mike Marable. He too by now was a Vietnam War veteran and working for a roofing company in Jefferson, Georgia. I stressed upon Nunny, Mike's mother, that I was counting on Mike to be there. She assured me she would take care of that detail and for me not to worry. When Mike returned home that evening, he received the "bombshell news." He was covered in tar and sweat from head to toe, but my red-headed best friend did not let me down. He was shining like a new penny and in his best attire when I saw him. He also had a great wedding present waiting for us after the ceremony.

After our pastor gave the benediction, Mike's girlfriend, Cathy Reese, Joan's sister, gave the oral wedding invitation. Mike and Joan waited behind the stage as all the seniors, including Cheryl, marched out.

Then as planned, Pastor Reese stayed on stage, and Mike and Joan appeared from behind the curtains from one side. The piano struck up the wedding processional and into the gymnasium walked my bride with our license. When Cheryl reached stage level, we both proceeded to our pastor from opposite sides to the center.

About half the graduation audience stayed to watch such an unconventional wedding. I'm sure some thought they would see a "shotgun wedding." I heard through the gossiping grapevine that our marriage would never work. All I can say to that is after forty-seven years, two children, and seven grandchildren, what did not work about it?

Far be it from me to take any credit for all the good things that came our way in the early days of our relationship as courting pairs, as fiancées, and as marriage partners. Feeling young and invincible does not run hand in hand with humility. It was quite easy to ignore my Invisible Friend and feel as if all this just happened as a result of our brilliant planning. As anyone with the faith of a mustard seed can see, there had to be a divine light guiding us to this inevitable bond. We were building upon the solid rock as the foundation for our lives together.

We gathered for pictures at court level and finally jogged down the gym floor and out the back as Mr. and Mrs. Billy Boyd Lavender. The surprise Mike had for us was to chauffeur us in his Ford Fastback Torino to where he had Mother's Impala hidden. Then we left for Gainesville, Georgia, for the first night of our forty-seven year honeymoon.

After our first night we decided to return home and stay at Mom and Dad's house for obvious financial reasons. The next two weeks would be a wonderful stay at the Hardigree/Haulbrook house, the only house and home I had ever known.

The time flew by, and I had to allow a few days to get back to Guam for my last six months of preferred sea duty. Cheryl would work at Reliance Electric with Mrs. Anderson until I was finished in Guam. I would have more leave time then. On a Sunday morning, Mom, Dad, Cheryl, and I went to Warner Robins Air Force Base to catch my MAC flight back to Guam. I checked in and began the wait for my flight to San Francisco. We said our goodbyes, and they returned to Watkinsville. They had left the base when the news of the flights delay came in. It would be a thirty-six-hour delay. I had my flight confirmation, but what was I going to do for thirty-six hours? I caught a bus home to Watkinsville and walked into the Sunday evening worship service at Antioch Christian Church and sat by my blushing bride. My parents so understood how I felt; they repeated that Sunday trip again on Monday.

I terminated my leave period at the MAC terminal in Hawaii and still had eighty hours to get to Guam. I arrived with time to spare.

# I Met My Heart in San Francisco

Roger and Sonia were not surprised that Cheryl and I were married when I returned, but they were very happy for us. The six months until October were now bearable for me. Since my brother and his family arrived on Guam approximately the same time I had, we would also receive orders for our transfer about the same time. With just a few months left, we were called "short timers." We would count the days down and mark them from the calendar.

Leaving for San Francisco, California, October 10, 1971

Warner Robins AFB, June 16, 1971

With about three months left, my brother and I both received our separate transfer orders. His next duty station was San Diego Naval Base, and my orders were to the U.S.S. Molala ATF-106, a fleet tugboat, homeported in San Diego. It was effectively an extension of brother duty. Roger was delighted. He had told me many times that to really learn my job well enough to get promoted, it would require time at sea.

Immediately after arriving back at the Nimitz Hill Message Center, the chief in charge put me in the AUTODIN room. That was short for automatic digital network. It was a room designated for a giant state-of-the-art machine. It was a computer that interfaced our ships at sea compatible with the teletypewriter. Even now, forty-five years later, I feel uncomfortable saying much more about it and the space where it was located.

Message handling is very precise and critical from the time it is received to the time of its delivery. Outgoing messages at the message center are time-stamped upon receipt and again upon transmission. All incoming messages for transmission are crudely drafted with an authorized releasing signature and have a classification and precedence. Optimally a routine is handled within a twenty-four-hour period. A priority is handled within six hours. An immediate is handled within thirty minutes. A flash is handled as fast as humanly possible or within five minutes. These handling instructions are observed throughout the navy on land and sea.

The colors of duplicating paper were pink for top secret, yellow for secret, green for confidential, and white for unclassified. The rule of a "need to know" coincided all handling instructions and the access into all secure spaces. Top of the Mar and the Nimitz Hill Message Center were very secure spaces. Combination entrances were everywhere. There were other spaces that I was cleared to enter for only the delivery of message traffic and keeping the cryptographic equipment secure on a daily basis. That is all I will say about that.

Once while training on the AUTODIN, the alarm for classification, plus some alarm I had never heard, activated. The communications watch officer (CWO) heard the commotion and stuck his head into the room to see if I was handling the message appropriately. He knew, in general, what the alarm meant, but he did not want to know specifically what the message contained; then it would be an added responsibility for him. I became weak in the knees when I read the header and saw the *top secret top category* classification from President Nixon at the White House. It was action addressed to his brother-in-law, Admiral Pugh. I thought I should relinquish the message to a higher-ranking and more experienced member of our watch section, but I was instructed by the communications watch officer to gather up the tape, attach it to the mat, make no copies of it, and follow its instruction.

The precedence was immediate, which meant the message needed to be delivered within thirty minutes. So I did as I was instructed. Dressed in my dungaree bell-bottoms, I rode the elevator up four floors to Admiral Pugh's office.

Outside his office was the office of his secretary. When I approached her desk, she asked. "May I help you?"

Gathering together the words that I should say, I was alarmed at what came from my mouth: "The admiral has a message from the president."

She immediately stood and said, "I'll see if he can see you."

To my relief, she immediately returned and said, "He'll see you."

She escorted me into his large office where the admiral sat leafing through papers.

No words were spoken at first as I handed him the message—a bundle of paper tape hanging from a mat—across the large desk where he sat. Relying on my basic training, I went to the position of parade rest. My Invisible Friend then spoke to me saying, "Do you see a man skillful and experienced in his work? He will stand in honor before kings; He will not stand before obscure men" (Proverbs 22:29).

When the admiral had finished, he handed me the mat and tape and said, "Destroy it."

I popped to attention and said, "Aye, sir!" I then left for the burn room.

On the way to the burn room, I had a couple of things on my mind. One was the extreme contrast between my chores this day and my chores back on the farm. The other was the question of whether I should read the message. Knowing that the message must have been drafted in Washington, DC, I presumed that no more than four or five individuals in the whole world would ever know its contents so I read it. From that afternoon until my honorable discharge seven years later, my security clearance became top secret special category—though it was never used in that capacity again.

Another secure space in close proximity to where I worked was the Fleet Weather Central. It was the weather center for every ship in the Western Pacific Ocean. These ships relied heavily on the weather maps that were transmitted from Nimitz Hill. A facsimile transmitter would transmit these maps on the locations of tropical depressions, tropical storms, and typhoons. The Fleet Weather Center also relied upon the barometric pressure readings and temperature readings the ships would send back to them. The Fleet Weather Central was filled with commissioned meteorologist and requested that a radioman be assigned to them for this specific job. I was assigned to work there. The duty was less stressful, but I did not get the diverse training I would need for promotion.

Once my brother and I had confirmed orders to San Diego, we could make plans for our arrival in California. Since Roger was an E-7 and career designated, he could have his 1967 Cutlass Supreme Oldsmobile shipped back to stateside. It was time for his family to buy another automobile more suitable for his growing family. I agreed to get a loan at the Navy Credit Union and purchase his Cutlass so Cheryl and I would have a means of travel when we met again in October.

Roger's flight out of Guam to San Diego came first by about twelve hours. I flew out on a separate flight with the rest of his family later that same day. Uncle Ralph was already living in San Francisco with his family. Grandmother Cleo was staying with Ralph in San Francisco for two weeks. Uncle Ralph, his family, and Grandmother Cleo were thrilled about the family reunion we planned to have upon our arrival from Guam.

# IT CAN'T BE LUCK

I remember standing in the customs line at the airport after I got off the jet. I could see Cheryl through the maze but could not reach her until my luggage had been checked and released.

It was a blessing to have loved ones to travel with across the ocean and relatives waiting on us when we arrived in San Francisco. Uncle Ralph took us directly from the airport to his home, and we settled in for the weekend. We needed that time to consider our personnel logistics concerning the arrival and transfer of the Cutlass into our procession. We then planned the long drive down the California coast to San Diego. Uncle Ralph and his family were great hosts. Cheryl and I slept in Uncle Ralph's camper in his back yard since he had to host six other family members. On the first morning of our stay, Grandmother Cleo showed me how she made biscuits.

My mother was the oldest of Grandmother Cleo's children. She married my dad in 1936, and Roger was born in 1937. Grandmother Cleo's last child was Uncle Ralph born that same year. That arrangement meant Grandmother Cleo was visiting with six grandchildren. Four were Uncle Ralph's children. Roger and I made up the other two. Roger's three children meant an additional three great grandchildren. While we were staying with Uncle Ralph, all fourteen of us visited Disneyland. Cheryl and I stayed close to Grandmother Cleo that day. She was seventy-three years young but still could not keep up with the main cluster of the family. It was a sunny warm day in October for Northern California. The top of Grandmother Cleo's head became hot and sunburned. Cheryl and I bought her a large strawhat with a broad brim to shield the sun from her head and shoulders.

On Monday Roger and I visited the vehicle compound where our 1967 Cutlass was stored. Once we had the vehicle in our possession, we were ready for our trip down the coast. What a wonderful time we had getting used to each other all over again. We literally drove the coastal highway all the way to San Diego. At times we could see the ocean down the steep bluffs and sea lions sunning themselves on the rocks below.

Once we were all in San Diego, Roger and I set about finding our respective suitable residences. Until Navy housing became available for Roger's family, they would live in a rented house across town. Cheryl and I rented our honeymoon cottage for $60. It wasn't much. It had a kitchenette, a small living room, a shower and toilet, and enough room for a double bed. It had gas heat. Only a curtain separated the bedding area and bathroom area. We had each other, so what else did we need? I was very happy. We were about ten to fifteen minutes from the pier where my ship was docked with her sister ships and some small destroyers.

One of our memorable moments was the day we selected to set up housekeeping. It was our first grocery-shopping trip to the Navy commissary. It obviously came early after our selection of the cottage. We were "rookies" to say the least. The only way we had to preserve many of our items was the small refrigerator in the cottage. We did not know that some groceries need refrigeration after opening. We did not make a list and bought first time items like salt and pepper, can openers, and knives that would not be purchased every time thereafter.

We spent $120 at the commissary. That bought two buggies full. Much of it spoiled, but we secured 90 percent of what we needed. Our receipt for the purchases was about six feet long and brought chuckles from the checkout clerks. We rolled it up in tight roll and stretched one of Cheryl's hair bands around it and saved it. We still have it.

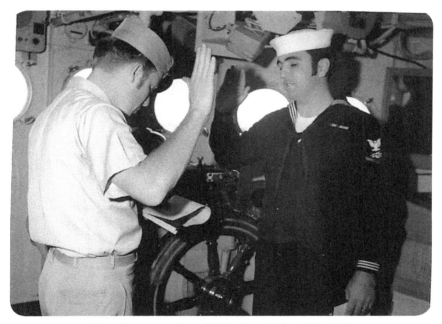

Reenlistment aboard U.S.S. Molala ATF-106

# U.S.S. Molala ATF-106

Almost everyone knows what a tugboat is and what they look like. They are not designed to be a majestic floating vessel loaded with a primary arsenal but are built for rugged service and towing. Its attributes are concealed in its powerful diesel engines that are geared for tremendous thrust to its stern and propeller.

The USS *Molala* was a fleet tugboat. It is one of the smallest seagoing ships the Navy has in its armada. The entire class of fleet tugboats is named after Native American Indian tribes. The Molala Indians were native to the Oregon territory but were forced to relocate in the early 1800s. This class of ship at the San Diego Naval Base was assigned to the Service Force Pacific Fleet.

It was 205 feet long and 38 feet wide. It had a crew of sixty-five sailors representing almost every major professional class of sailor from boatswain mate, electricians, engineman, yeoman, hospital corpsman, commissary men, signalman, to radioman. There were four major departments. The commanding officer and executive officer were in a class unto themselves. The engineering, operations, and deck department had their respective commissioned or warrant officer department heads. The commanding officer was most commonly a lieutenant, and the executive officer was a lieutenant junior grade. The operations officer was an ensign. A warrant officer headed the engineering and deck departments. They were given the respectful titles of captain or CO, XO, engineer, or boatswain. All were addressed with nothing less than a sir.

The ship had five levels. Below decks were the *hole* or engine room and berthing areas. Located on the main deck were the head, mess decks, and one five-inch gun, the yeoman, and hospital corpsman. Located on the 01 level were the commanding officer and the executive officer's stateroom. Next door to the XO's stateroom were radio central and the transmitter room. Up a ladder was the con where the helm and chart room were located. The smallest of the five levels was called the signal deck. That is where the signalman used his large lamp to flash messages to other ships on the horizon at sea.

The operations department had only three radiomen, so I was well received when I reported aboard. Three-section duty is 100 percent better than port and starboard duty. While the ship is at sea, communication is a twenty-four hours, seven days a week-type job. Port and starboard duty is twelve hours on and twelve hours off. Three-section duty is eight hours on and twelve hours off. My arrival meant four section duty and six-hour watches at sea. During normal working hours at sea, all radiomen worked in radio central. With four-section duty, it meant adequate rack time to rest and time to catch the movie on the mess decks in the evening.

The leading radioman was an E-6 career designated petty officer. When I arrived, radio central had two E-4 petty officer radiomen. I was still a radioman seaman, E-3. The leading radioman wanted to train and qualify for the Con, which would take some time away from his radio responsibilities. The entire radio crew was enthusiastic about getting me trained for radioman of the watch. I was a little intimidated at first, but with some time at sea I quickly adjusted.

Except for the short-term missions, the Service Force had for us, most of our extended missions out of San Diego were less than two weeks at sea. In 1972 we were assigned to assist NASA in test towing fuel fuselages that would be used in the new space shuttle program. The large fuel cells would be dislodged from the space shuttle high in the atmosphere and fall into the ocean. They had to be tested to see if the fall into the ocean and towing would weaken them and thus be unfit for reuse.

In 1972 we were homeported in Subic Bay, Philippines, for six months on a Western Pacific deployment. We were in and out of Subic Bay several times before an extensive duty tour in various western ports. There seemed to always be something for a fleet tug to do. We retrieved ships that had run aground. We towed barges. We positioned fleet weather buoys plus towed anything that needed towing. The various missions took us to Sasebo and Okinawa, Japan, Vietnam, and Bangkok, Thailand.

Toward the end of the 1972 deployment, we were granted R&R (rest and relaxation) in Hong Kong, China. The executive officer arranged a package deal to fly the wives of all the radiomen, his wife, and the COs wife to Hong Kong, China, for that week of R&R. I scratched and saved every dime I could so Cheryl could come to China. It did not leave much to send home to her, but I was hoping our time together would be worth the sacrifice. We had a wonderful week at the Hong Kong Hilton Hotel.

# Becoming the Complete Radioman

While in Danang Harbor, Vietnam, in 1972, the Viet Cong sappers were the largest threat to the U.S. Navy ships. Swimmers would swim below the surface and attach timed mines to the hull and swim away. The sun was setting, and I was authorized to hit the rack for the midwatch. This irritated some of the deck hands that radiomen seemed to get this preferential treatment. To appease his crew the boatswain delighted in dropping the first percussion grenade over the side right by my rack. I could touch the bulkhead with my hand from inside my rack. The water was on the other side of the bulkhead and so was the grenade. The explosion was jarring. I thought a sapper had mined us. I grabbed my blanket, and up the ladder I ran. When I ran onto the fantail half naked, my shipmates were cracking up with laughter. It took me a while to realize it was a prank. I did not get a wink of sleep the rest of the night as the grenades exploded at timed intervals to keep away the sappers.

Two days out of Vietnam, reports were broadcast that more than one dead sapper was found washed up near where we had been.

There were several occasions as radioman of the watch that called upon me to make some major decisions. The eight-hour watches required rigid discipline with the radio procedure that we were taught in school. The importance of the work radiomen did aboard ship become stressfully apparent while sitting the watch alone.

Some of the roughest weather I experienced as a sailor was in the waters around Sasebo, Japan. It was not uncommon for the Molala to pitch and roll in twelve-foot seas. That brought with it the usual motion sickness that at least 25 percent of the crew experienced. The higher the waves, the higher percentage of sicknesses was prevalent. No matter how salty or experienced the career personnel wanted you to believe they were, we all got sick at one time or the other. I remember getting sick twice, which was a pretty good record. One of those times was when the seas were in excess of fifteen feet. All the radiomen that I needed to turn to for assistance were in their racks with motion sickness, which only compounded my helplessness.

At any given moment when a ship was at sea in the Western Pacific, the commander of the Pacific Fleet would send out a flash message to get the location of a particular ship. We never knew when we would receive such a message. We must answer back within five minutes. The simple acknowledgment meant we were where we were supposed to be at that time. The weather was extremely rough when I received such a report. I ran to the transmitter room to set up the frequency for the transmission back to Hawaii. The Molala was pitching and rolling. I braced my feet against the bottom of the six-foot-tall transmitter with my buttocks pressed hard against the bulkhead and my elbows braced on the edge of the equipment. I tried to set the dials. Time was passing quickly, and the seas were not cooperating. I became sick, but that would be no excuse to go to the head while on duty with a flash message to transmit. A bucket and swab were located in the transmitter room beneath my knees. How convenient. I didn't even move the swab in the bucket before I lost my dinner. Then it was back to work, successfully answering within five minutes.

With rough weather also comes poor propagation. Selecting the best transmission frequencies and the best receiver frequencies was necessary for message clarity both for a TOD (time of delivery) and a TOR (time of receipt). The job was not complete until one time or the other was determined.

A shipmate had a bad infection in his foot. The corpsman had done everything he knew to do and had requested instruction from the Naval Hospital in Yokosuka, Japan. I sent the message in poor weather conditions, and the characters around the TOD was garbled, but I had accepted those type TODs before. However, in this case no answer to the sent message was received back in a timely fashion. The message was sent to Sasebo, but the hospital was in Yokosuka. At the

## IT CAN'T BE LUCK

time I knew I had good communications with Sasebo delivering all other message traffic.

I asked the XO if I could send a "service message" to check on the delivery of the original message.

He said, 'No!"

I was terribly worried about the possibility of my shipmate losing his foot. I went back to radio central and checked the TOD one more time. It was disturbing to me that I might be the cause of my shipmate's recovery or fate. I knew it would only take a minute or two if I bent the rules just a little.

Breaking radio procedure on the teletypewriter, I contacted a radioman at Sasebo and asked if he had a landline to Yokosuka. He answered back yes. I gave him the date/time/group of the message and asked him to check to see what happened to it. About two or three minutes went by before my teletypewriter started up for an incoming message. The radioman on shore turned the tables and made me net control and asked was I ready to receive a message. I had never done that before. In came the answer to the message I had delivered the prior week. The radioman on shore at Sasebo said that Yokosuka had literally dropped the ball, and the message had been lost. I thanked him and immediately processed it as an incoming message, and no one was ever the wiser about my disobeying the XO's order. The proper medication was given and my shipmate's foot was saved.

On one other occasion the XO and I were both up in the wee hours of the morning. We were arriving at the Port of Hong Kong, China, for our R&R. I had the midwatch and would be relieved at 0600 hours (6:00 a.m.). I would have about two hours to rest before meeting Cheryl on the pier. It was another very unusual situation.

The "broadcast" is how all ships in the Pacific Fleet receive message traffic. The incoming traffic of the broadcast is continuous and must be screened for any message traffic meant for any particular ship. On this occasion a message with a long address heading and the precedence of routine came in from the commander of the Pacific Fleet in Hawaii. Its only action addressee was the U.S.S. Molala. All the other addressees were for information only and contained all the other ships deployed in the Pacific Fleet. The message was therefore explicitly for the U.S.S. Molala. The proper handling procedure after normal hours was to take all action messages to the officer of the Con (the one navigating the ship). When I got to the bottom of the ladder leading to the Con, I saw the XO in his bathrobe at the top of the ladder.

He shouted down to me. "Lavender, what is the precedence of that message?"

I replied back. "Routine, sir!"

"Not now!" he retorted. "We have drifted into communist waters, and we have more important issues."

I went back to radio central and read the message. The reason it was action addressed to us was because we were the only U.S. Navy ship in the port. The date/time/group indicated it was over twenty-four hours old, which made it more urgent than a routine precedence since we were already on location. The text read, "Secure all transmitters while in the port." I hated to do it, but I returned to the Con. When the XO saw me on the pilot house, he became furious. He pushed me into the chart room with an expletive. His eyes were like daggers as he asked me what was so important. I was a little bit angry myself when I shoved the message into his gut. He glared back at me, and for a moment I thought he would strike me, but he read the message. He ordered me to show it to the leading radioman. I hated to awaken my supervisor, but I carried it to him with a flashlight in hand. He read it and simply said, "Secure all transmitters."

I must admit, I took great pleasure in returning to the Con and the transmitter room and shutting down all the transmitters for voice and frequency shift keying for the entire week we were there.

When I was relieved from watch duty, I told my relief we could only receive message traffic. We could not transmit anything for the entire week we were in Hong Kong. I then hit the rack for a couple of hours rest before meeting Cheryl.

At 0800 the XO held a personal reveille for me by my rack. I hopped to attention in my skivvies. The XO was shining like "new money." He was in his dress white uniform. Apologetically he said, "Lavender, I was wrong about last night." "Come on, the wives are on the pier!" "Let's have some fun!"

# IT CAN'T BE LUCK

Crossing the largest parts of the Pacific Ocean at twelve knots takes about ten to twelve days to Hawaii and then about that much more to ports beyond. I used the time at sea to fill out the practical factors for promotion to the next pay grade. It required having different officers to sign me off on general seamanship issues. Once the required time in grade had expired and the practical factors were completed, I would be eligible to take the E-4 examination for advancement.

Another time I bent the rules was two days after we had left Hawaii on our way back to San Diego. Both of our frequency-shift keying transmitters went down. The Molala was a WWII vessel and over thirty years old. After a rugged deployment, it seemed every department was having issues with casualty reports. The transmission message traffic backed up rapidly. Our leading radioman was the only one proficient at sending Morse code on the remaining transmitter that was operational. He ordered his three radiomen to cut the tapes and make the mats and keep them in one bundle in consecutive order. He would send what he could by precedence using Morse code, and the remainder could be carried to the message center when we arrived in San Diego, twelve days later. However, if we did have to deliver all that back traffic to the message center, and then wait on the responses to the requests, our liberty after a long deployment could be delayed. Having the ship restored to seaworthiness would be the first priority.

If the message traffic could be sent before arrival, everything necessary to restore the Molala to readiness would be waiting on the pier, and the departments could let their personnel go home or have liberty.

There were over thirty messages in that bundle of paper tape. With the transmission portion of the responsibility taken from us, the radiomen had a boring watch. Once again I stretched the envelope of discipline. I knew that the main transmitter was seriously down with a blown power amplifier. However, I was skeptical about the backup transmitter having that same problem. So I went into the transmitter room and checked it myself. I did what I had always done to set the frequency and power.

Properly tuned, the transmitters needed to show significant power forward, and a very small amount reflected back at the antenna. It was obvious that the backup transmitter had very low power; however, it tuned perfectly with five watts forward with no reflection. I thought some power is better than no power, so I set about making a plan for it to work. With the success I had in Japan, I thought I would try to connect with a radioman on shore that would help me. I was only going to try it one time, and if it did not work, I would be satisfied.

After tuning the backup transmitter perfectly, I taped the key down hard. Propagation was perfect. The sea was like glass. The skies were clear. It was my opinion that five watts could not possibly jam any particular frequency and all other ships could transmit over the top of my signal without my interference. But just maybe my signal would catch the eye of someone in San Francisco or San Diego and I could transmit.

It was about thirty minutes before I was to be relieved. I took down my *continuous key* and started to type. I explained our ship's casualty situation and crossed my fingers. Immediately the teletypewriter responded back with the proper "Q" and "Z" signals that my signal was clear and for me to send my traffic. I put up a five-second phase and shouted for the XO next door to come quickly. I flipped the switch as the XO looked over my shoulder at the communication I had made with San Francisco still ten days away. We held our collective breath as the long bundle dwindled down to the last message. Immediately San Francisco acknowledged receipt of all the messages except one, and I found its number and resent it. The XO was jumping up and down with both his hands on my shoulders saying, "Lavender, this is going to show up in your next evaluation!"

Soon after arriving back in San Diego, I was sent to take the E-4 examination for petty officer. As soon as the results were in, I had scored high enough for the first increment and received back pay. As a Navy tradition, new petty officers get their insignia "tacked on." That means all higher-ranking shipmates get to sock you on the arm where your insignia is attached. My arm stayed sore for a week.

Plaque/finalist, KSON 2nd Annual Country Star, January 13, 1973

# That Music Thing

The months following the deployment were wonderful for Cheryl and me. Everything felt right because we were together. Life was good. In the latter part of 1972, Cheryl attended the San Diego Key Punch Institute and received a diploma after six months. The year 1973 brought with it major decisions concerning our future and how we would make a living. We were a bit homesick for Georgia, and our families and my initial enlistment would be expiring soon.

The freedom of becoming a civilian again would allow me to focus on a recording contract, and that could be a means of income for us. San Diego was the home of KSON, the largest country and western radio station in America. For the year 1972 the station held an annual amateur show, but I could not participate in it because of the deployment. The winners of that show received a Capitol Records recording contract. The studios for Capitol Records were in Los Angeles. For 1973 KSON offered its Second Annual Amateur Show for another Capitol Records contract.

The timing seemed to be right. If I landed the contract I would be free from my first enlistment, and I could swap over to a music career. KSON advertised the amateur show regularly, giving the time and place for the auditions. The first year's winners were a group called The Brush Arbor. They were the judges for the second annual show. They were very complimentary about my audition.

The next week KSON announced the finalist on the radio while I was driving down the expressway. I nearly ran off the road when I heard my name as one of the finalists for the show.

The dates were set for rehearsal at the San Diego Civic Center with the concert orchestra. When the big night came, I shall never forget walking onto the stage after I was introduced to the 2,500

# IT CAN'T BE LUCK

members of the audience. The lights were blinding and hot. I could not see past the first two rows in the front, but I certainly could hear them cheering. Three of the members in the audience were the judges. They were the mayor of San Diego, the executive producer of *Hee Haw*, and Gene Autry.

For the same reason that I got a boisterous thirty-second ovation after each song may have been the same reason I did not place. I was introduced as a sailor from San Diego. I was a bit disillusioned with the appeal I seemed to have with the audience but still failed to place. My contract with the Navy may have been the issue. However, as time would prove, I had not consulted the giver of my talent, and I had tried in my own power to accomplish something that would not be good for our future.

After one year time in grade as E-4, I was eligible to take the examination for another promotion. I had already reenlisted and received my orders when I was sent for the exam. I remember a great many E-4 petty officers in the large auditorium. Most of these petty officers were scattered about throughout the middle of the room. All petty officers with security clearances were asked to select a booth with curtains that were located around the periphery of the auditorium. I really felt good about my chances of passing. I was familiar with almost everything they asked me.

Our choices were to leave the Navy and its financial security or reenlist and keep it. To entice qualified radiomen to sign up for another hitch, the variable reenlistment bonus was made available. For another four-year enlistment, the bonus was $8,600. For a six-year reenlistment, the bonus was $10,000. Both terms of reenlistment offered us our choice of orders.

After we considered our options as newlyweds, we could satisfy most of our wants and needs by signing up for four more years and choosing orders near home. We could then use the money to set up housekeeping properly.

The Naval Air Station in Albany, Georgia, was closing down by the first of 1974, and the personnel department wanted us to know it would be a short term of shore duty at that station. They would transfer us to the nearest shore station located near Albany after it closed if we signed up. The department also made us aware that officer's housing would be assigned to us in Albany since housing was becoming vacant and we had become career designated. We made the decision to transfer to the east coast and work near home for ten months and relocate to NAS Jacksonville, Florida, a short distance further south.

# Naval Air Station, Albany, Georgia

When the time for our transfer came, Roger and Sonia had planned a tour up the California Coast with our mom and dad who had come to visit. He and Sonia had purchased a large three-fourths-ton truck and camper for the trip, and we were invited to go. We stayed with them for the last few days we were in California and used the time to talk over our plans. We did not mean to disappoint anyone, but we had just completed three years of brother duty in the U.S. Navy, and Cheryl and I were ready to break ties and start out on our own. So after two or three days stay at their Navy housing, Cheryl and I struck out for Georgia.

The most difficult part of the trip occurred in the Mohave Desert. The air conditioner went out in the Cutlass, and the temperatures were around 120 degrees. We had to seek shelter and a mechanic. After repairs, we were back on the road for home and NAS Albany, Georgia.

In many ways those months of shore duty were really the best we ever had, but in some other ways not so good. By that I mean I began to learn the hard way, to my detriment and the detriment of our relationship how being blessed with so much effects the young unappreciative recipient. It is easy to become prideful and obtain a feeling of "the self-made man." I suppose this false pride is a part of growing up. It would have been a better time for us if I had chosen to acknowledge the provider of our blessing. Cheryl's Christian experience started when she was five years old. It was a genuine conversion, and she was wiser and had more years of experience than I walking the "Christian walk."

In Albany we received officer's housing right away. We loved the air-conditioned home with three bedrooms, complete bathroom, kitchen, hallway and large living room, a garage, and a significant yard with grass to mow. We purchased a mahogany bedroom suit, living room furniture, and a large color RCA TV console.

I checked in at the personnel office and then the NAS message center. I had a few more days off before I was to report for duty. When I reported in the afternoon around 1300 hours, the entire watch section and administrative personnel were lined up inside the message center and cheered me when I arrived. I was taken aback by such a welcome. They soon made it clear when Chief Swilley, the chief in charge, handed me a message that had come in over the broadcast. I had been promoted to E-5 with back pay effective immediately.

So like on the ship, my peers set about getting me trained for supervisor of the watch to make light duty even lighter for the rest of the watch section.

When I became fully trained in a week or two, I began to see how the other sections operated and followed suit. My leading radioman was an E-6. One night he had left me as the supervisor of the watch. That night about 0100 the midwatch was extremely slow, so I let the remaining three members of my watch section go home and took the watch alone. The bell rang at the entrance, and to my surprise a full captain wanted his message traffic. He was the commander of Reconnaissance Air Wing One. I promptly left for his traffic, but realized I had never met this high-ranking officer. That can work both ways. He could challenge me if I didn't challenge him.

When I returned I said as tactfully as I could, "Sir, I don't believe I have had the pleasure of meeting you. May I see your identification?"

He appreciated my tactful candor and immediately reached for his identification and slid it under the barred window.

Life was good in southern Georgia. Cheryl became pregnant with our only son, Joe, while we were in Albany. This was another area of our lives we had yet to experience together. I felt so helpless when I heard the echoing of Cheryl's morning sickness in the half vacant rooms of the house.

We also purchased two nice bicycles to ride over the large base. The automobile traffic was light, and the base seemed to expand over miles. It had a park and picnic area on Flint River where I had a pork BBQ for our department.

While in Albany Cheryl and I found a Jack Russell terrier puppy abandoned and gave it a home. We named her Daisy. It was a fiercely loyal and a protective female. Cheryl and I once went canoeing on Flint River. We secured Daisy in the Cutlass under the shade of a tree with the windows rolled down a bit at the top. Daisy was not happy. We felt sorry for her but thought it best if she stayed with the car. Apparently, the window was down too much, and she squeezed through the top and ran to the pier where we had just shoved off. Without slowing down and at a full run, Daisy ran off the end of the pier and swam to us. How could you not love a pet like that?

Even at the new pay grade and living in officer's housing with commissary benefits, Cheryl and I stayed financially broke most of the time because of our frequent trips home on the weekend. Cheryl's family and friends lived in Watkinsville and so did mine. I hunted and visited with my closest friends, Mike Marable and Edwin Bowden. The Vietnam War had changed Edwin, and PTSD shortened his life. Mike on the other hand has done very well, and we still are best friends. Though we never planned it in advance, Mike and I built each of our homes next door to each other. Mike eventually purchased forty acres on Oconee River across the road from our hill.

Chief Swilley sold us the mobile home he had lived in while at NAS Albany. He also had his Cessna pilots' license, so we flew over to Valdosta to have the title's switched. I did not realize what a precarious situation I had put myself in until we took off. He had not flown in a while and wanted to stay qualified, so he had to have the take-off and landing instructions read to him. It was a shaky take-off and much more of a rocky landing. We bounced halfway down the runway coming into Valdosta. I was thankful to be on the ground but frankly dreaded having to repeat the ordeal again upon returning to Albany.

Officer's housing, NAS, Albany, Ga. 1973

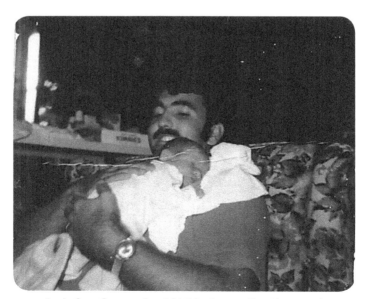

Joe's first few weeks, NAS Jacksonville, Fla. 1974

# IT CAN'T BE LUCK

Joe, NAS Jacksonville, Ga. 1974

Mr. and Mrs. Anderson's house, 1975

# Naval Air Station, Jacksonville, Florida

We visited Jacksonville, Florida, and the area around the base to find a place to put our mobile home nearby. On Collins Road there was a very nice mobile home park with accommodations. It had a pool and strict yard requirements. All of the tenants seemed to take pride in their yards and so did we.

After our ten months at the Naval Air Station in Albany, we packed much of our personal belongings into and onto our Cutlass Supreme. We looked like the *The Beverly Hillbillies* moving to Hollywood. Two bicycles on the rear bumper, a boat rack with numerous house items on top of the car and packed with pets and clothing on the inside. The Navy moved all other household items.

When we were settled into our mobile home I checked in at the personnel department and the message center where I would be working. NAS Jacksonville was busier than what I had been used to. The message center was much larger and more modern. As with every prior duty station, my immediate peers were glad to see me coming. It always meant relief at whatever duties they were performing. The leading radioman in my watch section at NAS Jacksonville was also an E-6. He had plans of becoming the communications watch officer after qualifying me for supervisor of the watch.

Cheryl and I soon made friends with other married Navy couples. One couple was from Lavonia, Georgia. Another couple was our next-door neighbors, and they also worked at the Naval Air Station.

# Another Chance at Music

The disillusionment I had experienced since the amateur show in California still haunted me. An advertisement came over the WJAX radio station in Jacksonville. It was the second largest country and western music station in America. It was the mirror image of KSON. After an audition, this advertisement, however, offered an opportunity to cut a record in the Nashville studios. Since the amateur show, I had not given up on the possibility of a breakthrough, provided that the right individual or group of people could hear me sing. I auditioned and was told by that person that I fit the criteria for what the label was seeking. He did not hide the fact that I needed to sponsor some of the expense in order to make it happen. I thought it was fair then and understood the terms that I agreed to.

The producer of the record label had ties to the music industry. Cheryl was OK with the idea, but she was putting more trust in me than anything else. I got the feeling she had some skepticism about it all. It may have been the pregnancy and me leaving for a few days as much as anything. Joe was not due until July, and this was the early part of 1974.

I arrived in Nashville, Tennessee, after driving straight through. The weather was noticeably cooler the farther north I traveled. I called the producer as soon as I arrived. We chatted on the phone for a short while as I settled into my motel room for the night. The next morning, he picked me up on time in his black Cadillac and took me to his office where we went over the plan.

He had a credenza full of prerecorded musical accompaniment that had already been produced in the studios. He also had the lyrics to a large assortment of unrecorded possibilities. He wanted to hear some of my original compositions and began to take notes.

He wanted to use some of my original songs, but I did not like the changes he was making to them. I was not ready for that. He then let me hear some of his musical library. All I had to do was put my voice with the lyrics to the music. I knew I could do that. The musical accompaniments were all the parts of the conventional country band with drums, steel guitar, bass, lead guitar, backup singers, etc. Violins would be an additional feature if I decided to add them later.

I chose two songs entitled "Liberated Woman" and "Kentucky Girl." I would replace the voice that was initially put on one of the tracks. I was impressed with his work and decided that it would be the "A" and "B" sides to the 45-rpm vinyl record we would produce. The producer gave me a cassette player with the tape and sent me back to my room to learn the lyrics. He told me to let him know when I was ready. I called him the next morning.

The producer was skeptical that I could have it down so soon and asked me to sing them in his office. The studio time was expensive and so were the recording engineers. Everything needed to be close to perfect to cut down on the studio time. I showed him what I could do. He was impressed and immediately called the engineer to meet us. The time was about nine in the morning, and it was cold outside. We drove in separate cars, and I followed him there. I did not expect to spend another night away from Cheryl.

Inside the studio in a soundproof room were the microphones. The engineer sat behind a large glass window at the controls. "Kentucky Girl" was a "take" the first time through. "Liberated Woman" was almost perfect too, but he wanted a rerun through a line or two. That was it. About ten minutes inside the same studio that had recorded "Little Green Apples," and I was done.

About 10:00 a.m. I was finished. I sat in the car for a moment and caught my breath. It was time to go home. The snow started to fall, and I was so lonely for Cheryl.

The agreement would allow me to receive five hundred copies of the record to use in my own promotion efforts. His obligation was to send the record to the top five hundred country music radio stations in America. No guarantees other than that. If the disc jockeys played it and it took off, it would be reflected in the Billboard

Charts. The record label of my first and only vinyl 45 was RELCO. If it made a billboard response, I would be offered a major label. The only deficiency in the agreement may have been its lack of promotion. The producer was being careful to get a feel for how well the record performed before he expended the promotional cost.

It seemed like a long period of time before my records finally came to me. I put a few records on consignment at the record shops in Athens, Georgia. I began visiting every radio station I could drive to for live interviews, etc. WNGC, North Georgia Country, in Athens, Georgia, gave me a live interview over the air when I took them the record. WDOL in Athens was strictly a twelve-hour AM country station and played my record frequently the day I took it to them. In fact, they signed off the air with the commentary, "By far the most requested record we have played today has been Watkinsville's own Billy Boyd Lavender's debut record, Liberated Woman." That particular week after my local record release, I was #19 with "Liberated Woman." Elvis Presley's record "Danny Boy" was #20. All of that was relative and ludicrous. It made me chuckle.

It was a fun time for me. To hear my record played over the airwaves was a lifelong dream that was finally coming true. But once again I had tried to do this music thing in my own power. I had not asked God's blessings nor did he give them to me. I learned later in life he had done this for a good reason.

It was imperative that I get my record played on WJAX. One Saturday morning I made it my mission to take my record to the station. I could see the radio tower but was having an extremely difficult time finding the right road that would take me to it. A bit exasperated I pulled into an office complex and knocked on the door of a local business. The owner of an advertising agency came to the door. After a quick introduction, I asked him how I could get to the radio station. He explained to me how to get there. After I got his directions, I thanked him and awkwardly gave him a copy of my record as a token of my thanks and hurried back to the car.

Before I got in the car, he called out. "I'll listen to it. How do I get in touch with you?"

I thought that was odd, but I gave him our phone number and left.

WJAX made no promises. They said if the music director liked it he would probably put it on the air early in the mornings before the peak airtime. That was good enough for me. I went back to work at the message center on Monday. When I arrived back at home Cheryl told me the man at the advertising agency had called. Frankly his name hardly rang a bell. He wanted me to call him right away. Cheryl explained he was the president of Atkinson Advertising Company and wanted me to discuss my record with him. I was very curious about his interest and returned his call. He gave me directions to his mansion and had me over.

We discussed my contractual ties with RELCO, which were none. He made it clear he was an instant fan and wanted to promote me. I was very grateful but really skeptical about what was in it for him. Every time I showed my concern about the cost of his promotional plans, he would tell me not to worry about it. He told me it was part of his business to win some and loose some. I assumed by that he was saying he could write it off. I told him I was in the Navy and that would have to come first. He understood and asked me if I could work after hours with his commercial artist, but I had no transportation. Cheryl had started to work at Blue Cross and Blue Shield and was using our car after she dropped me off at work.

Atkinson Advertising provided me a Volkswagen to drive to and from his office after working in the message center. I was to compile a mailing list of the top five hundred country and western stations in America. To do this he provided a "fine-printed catalogue" about three inches thick with every station in America. I did it.

In the meantime his commercial artist designed a lavender envelope with silver swirls and stars to ship my record to these stations. We needed a promotional picture to enclose with the record. He sent me to a designer store to purchase an outfit for the photograph. Cost did not seem to be an issue. The day came for the photograph. He gave me his wife's brand new Corvette Sting Ray sports car to drive downtown Jacksonville to the professional photographer's studio. I certainly looked the part, if nothing else.

Consistently I was told not to worry about what it cost. He was so sure the record would hit; we would talk that over then.

Promotional picture, 1975

# The Birth of Joe and My Rededication

It was July 16 when I came home, and Cheryl was not there. Joe was due at any time. Of course I was concerned and set about looking for her. I found her next door sitting with the neighbor's wife. Their child was about a year old.

I looked at her for a few seconds to get a feel for what was going on. Liz, the neighbor, explained that Cheryl had a few pains, and they were talking it over. Like all expectant fathers for the first time, I was at a loss. The pains were too far apart to be of concern, but you couldn't make me believe it. About sundown we drove to Naval Hospital on base. It took what seemed forever for them to see Cheryl, but the end result was false labor. False labor! Nine months pregnant, and they say false labor? She was not admitted. I was too concerned to go home, so they recommended that we walk until Cheryl dilated enough for admission. That was a difficult thing for us to do.

It was a long night. In the wee hours of the morning on the July 17, 1974, they finally admitted her. Cheryl was in more pain than I could bear to see. I wished I had gone to classes to take the edge off my anxiety. I could not get my mind around the miracle of birth. Cheryl was so small, and I was so frightful. In earnest I prayed and prayed.

Eighteen hours later, the nurse brought out our firstborn. He was red and wrinkled, twenty-one inches long and weighed seven and one-half pounds, but he was beautiful.

A change had come over me. I had turned to my Invisible Friend for help, and he had once again delivered. I was beginning to feel ashamed for having neglected him so much over the last few years. He began calling me back to him. I was so stubborn and afraid

I would have to give up something when actually I would gain much more by surrendering to him.

Because Cheryl and I were both working, there were times we needed someone to watch Joe. We found an elderly couple in the mobile home park, and they fell in love with Joe. They agreed to watch him for a small fee. I remember how helpless I felt when they had taken Joe with them to shop. It made me feel like I was abandoning my responsibility. It was a very uncomfortable feeling. They were good child caretakers however. Another uncomfortable feeling was when Cheryl started to attend Collins Road Baptist Church a few blocks away. She pleaded with me regularly to go with her, but I seemed to always have some poor excuse not to go. I started to miss her in a strange way. I wanted her to be with me, and I wanted to be with her, so I reluctantly decided to go to appease the entire situation.

It was August of 1974. Joe was just over a month old and at the babysitters. I decided to go to the bible study at Collins Road Baptist Church. They were studying the book of Revelation. The moment I stepped out of the car, my Invisible Friend came running to me. In a spiritual way it was similar to the meeting Cheryl and I had at the airport in May of 1971. His love for me was expressed differently by saturating my soul with the unseen attributes of his creation. The fragrance of the evening honeysuckle blindsided me. I began to tremble, and before Cheryl could take my hand, my Invisible Friend engulfed me from head to toe. The crickets, dove, and whippoorwill joined in their harmonious song right on queue. The peace of the dusty roads from back home filled my being. I could not speak, and tears filled my eyes. Cheryl knew what was happening, and I'm sure she was saying, "Sic him, Lord!"

We entered the church and participated in the study. There were hardly twenty-five people present. At the end of the study period, the pastor gave an invitational prayer. My head was bowed, and my knuckles had turned white from gripping the pew in front of us. At the end of the prayer I went forward and rededicated my life to Jesus Christ. This was a genuine rededication. The bible became the answer to so many things I had wondered about.

...ible study kept me in the *word*. I found read-
...teresting. The Holy Spirit became my inter-
... something confusing, I learned it was the spirit
...ring. If I were faithful to ask the Lord to help my
...e would not allow the confusion to occur but pro-
... wisdom.

... ame another talent he had given to me. I had fallen so far behind in spiritual discernment he allowed me to catch up by helping me understand the prophetic riddles found in the book of Revelation. Whatever seemed confusing to me in Revelation could be clarified somewhere else in the Bible.

The personal Bible Antioch Christian Church had given to me as a high school graduating senior would go with me around the world. The Revised Standard Version with a concordance was invaluable for cross-referencing scripture. For me the Bible became the language book of God.

# One Thousand Records for Promotion

RELCO and Atkinson Advertising were both key players in the promotion or the lack thereof, of "Liberated Woman" and "Kentucky Girl." If they could have combined their efforts for the success of the record, it may have turned out differently. Indirectly the end game would have been the same if they had pulled together instead of exhausting each other's individual efforts.

As I recall the minimum quantity of records that could be pressed into vinyl was one thousand. Five hundred copies went for the initial RELCO promotion. RELCO would send out five hundred to the top radio stations in America. He encouraged me to use my five hundred for promotional purposes as well. As a result, the advertising agency and I replicated RELCO by using my five hundred in the same manner. However, Atkinson Advertising exceeded RELCO's promotion by way of photography and flashy envelopes, etc.

It was a fun time for me. I had relatives living all over the United States. Their eyes and ears were helpful in providing feedback and personal scouting reports. It was difficult to know if the stations that played my record were using the records that RELCO sent or the ones Atkinson Advertising sent. It didn't really matter so long as the listening public responded. The problem occurred when there was no record consignment by the record label. If the fans went to the record shop to buy my records, they were not there for purchase. What RELCO wanted was a narrow channel of feedback to Nashville with an overwhelming response before the producer sent more vinyl copies to those areas.

From my personal means of feedback, my record was played in twenty different states. On more than one occasion, I heard it played randomly on different stations in a few of those states. In a very personal way it felt to me that I was being teased each time I tried to break through into the music industry. The public response was always more than adequate. Each time I reached for my dream, disillusionment soon followed.

As with all children, their "wants" seldom match their "needs." Good parents will not withhold any good thing from their children if it is in their power to supply that good thing. I was learning a lesson from the giver of every good and perfect gift. He knew things about Cheryl and me and our marriage that a musical career would destroy. What the future held was unseen and unknown to us, but our Heavenly Father could see very clearly what lay ahead. He would provide a guiding light for both of us *through the valley of the shadow of death* several times throughout the years ahead.

I knew the time of our eighteen-month tour of duty at NAS Jacksonville would soon be coming to an end. I was becoming concerned about the cost the advertising agency was putting toward the promotion of the record. I would soon be receiving transfer orders to unknown parts of the world. It seemed he was throwing his money into a dark hole. Once again, he encouraged me and asked me to request an extension of duty at NAS Jacksonville.

I at least owed him that much, so I wrote a letter in earnest to the Bureau of Naval Personnel requesting an extension of duty. I stated that my transfer orders would be the seventh command in as many years.

The answer from the personnel department was one short statement. "Your request for extension of duty at NAS Jacksonville, Florida, would be unfair to contemporaries at sea."

I shuttered to think what that meant. When my transfer orders came in, it became quite clear.

# LCU-1661

I was assigned to Assault Craft Unit Two in Little Creek, Virginia. An assault craft unit is that portion of the Navy that provides smaller craft for the transfer of arms, equipment, and personnel to beachheads such as in Normandy on D-Day. These smaller craft are also known as landing craft.

While we were still in Jacksonville in the fall of 1975, Cheryl became pregnant with our daughter, Susan. We managed to sell the mobile home where it sat and left shore duty in Jacksonville for our last duty station in Little Creek, Virginia.

Starting again in Little Creek, Virginia, was like a fresh start. My perspective on life in general had taken on a more Christian tone than in the previous fifteen years. We purchased a new mobile home and set up our address in a park a short distance from the base.

The commanding officer of Assault Craft Unit Two was a full commander. The entire command utilized Quonset huts for all of its departments. Along the shoreline at Little Creek, Virginia, the Quonset huts were inland adjacent to where the landing craft were moored.

There were many landing craft designs for the many different needs during a beach assault. The one thing they all had in common was providing transportation over that margin of seawater between the amphibious ship and the beachhead or shoreline. In most cases the ship stayed off shore a safe distance to avoid beaching. On the other hand, the landing craft were designed to beach at full speed. The forecastle for all these craft had a heavy-duty ramp approximately the same width of craft to off-load equipment and personnel.

"Standby for beaching" was a command I would hear often in the coming months. It was a command no one aboard took lightly.

The craft would slide to an abrupt halt from twelve knots to zero in a second or two. For the upcoming deployment, my landing craft had a tank and a two-ton personnel transport secured to its deck with heavy chains which had to be immediately unsecured to allow a speedy disembarkation.

Most landing craft are of the smaller-type versions carrying a squad of personnel or maybe a jeep and small amounts of necessary supplies. The top of the line design for landing craft was the landing craft utility. In 1975 I was assigned to the LCU-1661.

It was a ten million-dollar craft with a ten-man crew. Most of its sailors were career designated. For the officer in charge (OINC) it required an E-6 ranking at a minimum. However, the highest-ranking OINC on these assault craft was a master chief petty officer, E-8.

Aboard LCU-1661 BM1 Ernest Houston was the man in charge. I was the next most senior ranking member of the crew, though E-5 Engineman Stacowitz provided the proper chain of command. The rest of the crew included an E-5 electrician, an E-5 boatswain mate, an E-5 commissary man (cook), an E-4 engineman, an E-3 engineman, and two E-3 seaman.

We were a tight crew. Below the main deck was a smaller version of a berthing area with personal lockers. Two hatches provided entrances into two other compartments. One was the lounge area where a reefer stored a month's supply of seaworthy goods. On one end of the lounge was the administrative hutch with a desk and a typewriter. Through the other hatch was the OINC's stateroom for BM1 Houston. The administrative hutch was where I spent much of my time drafting correspondence back to the unit in Little Creek.

The engine room was also below the main deck. The LCU was 120 feet in length and 23 feet across. There were two levels on the main deck though they rapidly diminished in size. In the small cabin area where the radios were housed were also the helm and the entrance to the ladder leading to the berthing area. Through the hatch and behind the helm was the mess deck with eight swing-out seats on the starboard side. On the port side of the passage was the mess deck equipped with the state-of-the-art cooking equipment for our fantastic commissary man, the cook. Through another hatch at the end of the mess deck were the head and shower.

Immediately above the helm, radio, mess deck, and head was the captain's chair. In front of his chair was a voice tube through which he shouted commands to the helmsman and enginemen for every beaching. On that level the antennas to my radios were also located.

It was apparent to me from the beginning of my assignment how necessary but dangerous and expendable these craft were. The many documentaries showing these landing craft under fire concerned me. The upcoming deployment to the Mediterranean would further help me to decide the future for my family.

The rest of 1975 was pleasant for us in Little Creek. I started selling Kirby vacuum cleaners and did well enough to obtain one for our own usage at virtually no cost. We enjoyed living in our new mobile home. I read the Bible regularly. We could not seem to settle into a local church. Cheryl and I both yearned for Antioch, and nothing could fill that void but the grand old church and community back home in Georgia.

The same time I was rededicating my life to Christ in Florida, BM1 Houston was also refreshing his walk with the Lord in Virginia. It was becoming obvious to me that he was making preparation for our mission overseas. Houston lived off base with his wife and family. As he learned more about my religious convictions, he asked Cheryl and me over for dinner at his house. He pointed out that he had not extended invitations to any of the other members of his crew. One of the reasons he had us over was to ask me to act as a chaplain for our small crew during the upcoming deployment to the Mediterranean. We both knew I was not qualified, but I did agree to do what I could for the spiritual needs of our team.

Houston and I discussed the more intimate details of our lives and also bounced scriptural references and questions off each other. He was careful not to get too close to the other members of the crew because of his authority over them. I appreciated his trust in me. While we were still in port at Little Creek, he would give me his thoughts on the communication back to the unit, and I would dress it up in a business letter and let him proofread it before mailing it back to Little Creek.

The first six months in Little Creek flew by fast, and time for the 1976 deployment came up rapidly. Cheryl was six months pregnant with our daughter, Susan. When our last night together came sometime in January of 1976, we unfolded the sofa and made it into a bed and watched television together into the wee hours of the morning. Cheryl wept on my shoulder all night. My T-shirt was wet from her tears. It was a miserable night for both of us, but there was no other place in the world we wanted to be but in each other's arms.

Sleeplessly she drove me to the pier. As with all previous deployments, upon arrival, the engines were fired up, and the smell of diesel smoke permeated the morning air. It was a sickening smell mixed with the lack of sleep that made for a sad and dismal departure. We said our one last tearful goodbye before sunrise, and I reported aboard LCU-1661 for seven long months at sea.

Cheryl had my blessings to return to Georgia for that period. With the birth of Susan in March, our families in Watkinsville would be of tremendous support for her and Joe in my absence.

Assault Craft Unit Two in Little Creek was an independent command until its services were required for TAD (temporarily assigned duty) to the larger amphibious forces. Two of the amphibious ships in the sixth fleet that were similar in design and usage were the U.S.S. Raleigh LPD-1 and the U.S.S. Spiegel Grove LSD-32. Both ships had well decks and a landing dock. For TAD, Assault Craft Unit Two assigned two of its LCUs and numerous other smaller landing craft to the 1976 deployment to the Mediterranean. LCU-1661, LCU-1654, and the smaller landing craft would literally catch a ride across the Atlantic Ocean aboard these two ships as part of the larger sixth fleet.

The LCU's main function was an amphibious assault craft; however, it can provide unique functions for various contingencies as would be proven in the 1976 deployment. A LCU is literally the smallest seaworthy craft in the U.S. Navy fleet. It can stay self-sufficient at sea for a month at a time. To maintain this type of readiness, our crew had trained up and down the Jersey shoreline several days at a time before the deployment.

The well decks of the Spiegel Grove and the Raleigh are identical in the nature of their design. The aft port and starboard compartments are deliberately flooded to sink the rear end of the ships to simulate the beaching maneuver. The landing craft are driven inside the flooded well deck area. The flooded area is then immediately pumped back into the ocean creating a "high and dry draft" of the lesser vessels inside the "well deck." The crew aboard the LCU rapidly secures the craft to the well deck of the larger ship with large chains identical to the way the LCU secured its cargo. The links in these chains weigh approximately seven pounds each. At the general quarters' command, this routine is reversed. If any of the large chains are not removed in a timely fashion, they are left and broken by the buoyancy of the LCU. That is really something to see and hear.

These chains are crisscrossed forward and aft port and starboard to keep the landing craft from shifting in heavy seas. Heavy equipment such as bulldozers, tanks, and two-ton trucks are also secured in this manner aboard the craft.

Once our craft was secured aboard the Raleigh, BM1 Houston met in his official capacity with the captain of the U.S.S. Raleigh to discuss duty assignments. Houston was successful in explaining how necessary it was for the crew to stay aboard the landing craft during the deployment to maintain our normal duty sections and the readiness of the craft. When the captain realized we were a small unit able to sustain ourselves, he allowed us to stay aboard LCU-1661. We connected sewage to the outside and tapped into the electrical grid of the ship with a large service drop cord. This was an amicable situation since the Raleigh housed 1,700 Marines plus its own crew. However, we did take advantage of chow on the Raleigh mess decks.

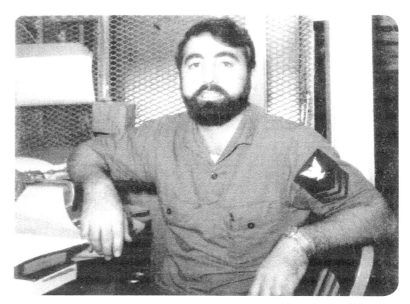

RM2 Lavender, 1976, leading radioman, landing craft utility, Assault Craft Unit Two, joint allied operations

# A Strange Occurrence in Palermo, Sicily

Twenty-one days later the sixth fleet sailed through the Strait of Gibraltar. For three weeks we had not seen land, but as we approached the strait, we first saw the Rock of Gibraltar. After we had sailed another two hours, we could see land on the port and starboard sides. It was the gateway to the Mediterranean Sea.

As soon as we hit port for refueling and restocking our supplies, we would be on our way again. In Rota, Spain, LCU-1661 was allowed to disembark the Raleigh and was given a short period of liberty. The crew was put under strict liberty restraints. All personnel, including the Raleigh sailors, were not allowed to go outside a confined area and for a good reason.

I agreed to take the duty aboard LCU-1661 so the crew could go over and have a beer. I was expecting to have the duty at least until the next morning. However, about six hours into liberty call, it was terminated, and all personnel had to return to their duty stations. We secured our craft once again inside the well deck of the U.S.S. Raleigh and continued on. Apparently the crisis in Beirut, Lebanon, was heating up.

Marseilles, France, was one of the only ports in which we were given any liberty at all. It was a moderately large city with its modern and historic features. It was basically cleaner than the only other port we visited in Palermo, Sicily.

As a young boy one of my favorite black and white thirty-minute episodes on TV was *Highway Patrol*. Almost anyone living through that era remembers its star, Broderick Crawford. In 1976 the actor would have been seventy years old. I and two other crewmembers were on liberty call on the streets of Palermo. It was an old port city in the Province of Sicily. There were no bars or pubs in the section of the city we were in. Looking for a place to light and have a beer or two before returning to the ship, we had to settle for a small restaurant on a cobblestone street in the old city.

Inside there were a very few tables with chairs around them. The smell of the wine in wooden barrels was prevalent. The owner had no beer for sale and was about to close; however, he did serve us a pitcher of wine. He had to climb his handy ladder up to the level where the barrels were racked. He turned the wooden spout and filled our pitcher. There was only one other man in this small venue. He wore an old soiled overcoat. He had been an American citizen and seemed anxious for our company. He offered to be our interpreter. As soon as he spoke, the obvious became mysterious. Not only did he have the balding and receded hairline and statue of Broderick Crawford, but also when the gruffness in his voice was heard, I began to wonder if I was in the presence of the actor himself.

The man seemed to have nothing to hide for he appeared to be at the end of himself. He answered all my nosey questions. Though he did not deny that he was indeed Mr. Crawford, he told us his story. His story was one of the mob and exile from the United States. I had no reason to doubt the stranger and was quaintly aware of Palermo's ties to organized crime.

The owner of the café was anxious to close around midnight, so the stranger invited us to his home a block or two away. We were intrigued but cautious. Just as he had said a block or two away between two buildings was what appeared to be a closed alleyway. It was no more than six feet wide and maybe twenty feet deep. At the very back was a filthy commode and sink. About ten feet inside from the sidewalk, a single bunk was hard pressed against the wall. There may have been a chair and a stool. I sat on his bed with him. He showed us some of his magazines in the dim light from a lantern and candle. He had a very poor and nasty existence. It was a strange evening.

We bid him a good night and farewell and returned to the U.S.S. Raleigh about one in the morning. Soon the ship was underway again. This time we stayed at sea except for joint allied operations with the Italian Navy.

## IT CAN'T BE LUCK

We beached in Sardinia, Sicily. It was a remote place with nothing to do but mix with other foreign sailors. On March 14, 1976, I had the duty. The other crewmembers were visiting the foreign craft that had less strict rules for alcohol and the use of it. One of our seamen became intoxicated and started a scuffle with an Italian sailor who was armed with a knife. The scuffle broke out on the main deck of our craft. Since I had the duty, it was incumbent upon me to handle the situation.

My shipmate was past the point of complying with my orders, so I grabbed the seamen by the collar and manhandled him to the back hatch. He would not step up and over, so I threw him through the hatch. He hit the metal deck harder than I had intended, but it broke up the skirmish. In the process I severely jammed my left big toe against the bulkhead. It was injured severely enough that BM1 Houston wanted it x-rayed. I was medevac'd to the Raleigh by boat and given several days rack time.

On the evening of March 15, 1976, Cheryl was having her favorite supper of fried chicken, greens, mashed potatoes, and all the other trimmings with my mom and dad at the Hardigree/Haulbrook house in Watkinsville, Georgia. By her own admission of having eaten too much food, her uncomfortable feeling was compounded with labor pains. Eight hours later, Susan was born. Cheryl said she cried when she first saw Susan. When I asked why she cried, she said because she looked just like me.

Yeah, no wonder she cried. Susan was really a beautiful baby though. She would later become one of the most beautiful Marine Corp females to wear the uniform. She would be three months old before I could see her for the first time.

On March 16, 1976, I was absorbing the rack time on the doctor's orders when another scuffle broke out on the main deck. I could clearly hear that something had happened. The noise subsided by my rack when down the ladder came all of my shipmates. The first in line to congratulate me was the seamen that had caused the insurrection two nights before. The entire crew was by my rack shouting. "It's a girl!" It's a girl!" I regretted that I was not standing by my radio to receive the news firsthand. But the relay of the voice message transferred from the U.S.S. Raleigh by my shipmates made it the happiest day of 1976 until the end of the deployment.

Of the seven months I was away from home in 1976, six months of that time was spent at sea. The eight years I had obligated to Uncle Sam seemed to Cheryl and me to be a career's worth of travel and experience. My separation from Cheryl and the children began to weigh heavily upon my future decisions for the family. The guiding light provided by my rededication to Christ caused me to study the Bible regularly and to seek his answers for our future.

There was a very real difference in the direction I sought for our lives now, than in the previous seven years. The responsibility of a family now entered the equation, plus some important unseen factors. Cheryl and I began to take life a day at a time. We cautiously applied Proverbs 3:5–6: "Trust in the Lord with all your heart and lean not on your own understanding; in all your ways submit to him, and he will make your paths straight."

Once again we were embarked on the U.S.S. Raleigh LPD-1. The well deck at times reminded me of the belly of a whale (Jonah 1:4–6). It was obviously a much cleaner and organized existence than Jonah's ride in the big fish. I utilized that time at sea for Bible study and begin to write about all the jumbled emotions I felt inside. I sought desperately to express what I was feeling.

I wrote a long manuscript that I entitled "Around the Opened Eye." It was easy to become self-aggrandizing for an amateur writer. I thought I had finished the manuscript and wanted someone else to see what a great work I had done. I discovered that the chaplain, a full captain, was also a writer. He invited me to his stateroom where I rendered my work. He was very gracious and agreed to edit my manuscript.

When he had completed the edited the manuscript, I was figuratively smacked in the face. It was like an essay back in school. It had been marked with red ink. There was much to learn within those red marks. On a positive note he admitted that he enjoyed reading about my family. He gave me another editorial truism I never forgot. He told me a writer must write as if the reader is a guest looking over his shoulder and watching every word he jots down. Do not offend them nor forget their presence and treat them with the upmost respect. I kept the manuscript in a notebook and continued to use it for the purpose of taking notes and used it as a study guide. Learning to discern God's will for my life became a passion. The more I studied the scriptures, with more clarity they spoke to me. I was beginning to see the guiding light directing me away from the military service. Cheryl and I trusted God's word from Proverbs 16:3: "Commit your work to the Lord and your plans will be established."

# Beirut, Lebanon, 1976

Stealthily the sixth fleet moved closer to the war torn area of Beirut, Lebanon. The several different factions that controlled the area had closed down all avenues for the American citizens to evacuate. No highways were open, no airports were allowing flights, and no means of travel allowed the American citizens to leave. The only means of evacuation for the American citizens from Beirut, Lebanon, was by sea.

In the operations order for our deployment, that contingency in the operations order was the responsibility of the LCU-1661. I immediately felt the pressure. Assault Craft Unit Two had come to the forefront of a world crisis. Our craft was designated in the op order to move into Beirut and receive the American citizens aboard LCU-1661 and then transport them back to the U.S.S. Raleigh or the U.S.S. Spiegel Grove.

The tension ran high among our crewmembers as the inevitable was presented. BM1 Houston held an all hands meeting to explain the importance of our mission.

As directed by President Ford, Secretary of State Henry Kissinger, and the joint chiefs of staff, we were to arrive at the pier in Beirut with no show of force. That meant to slowly enter and moor our craft with our scant weaponry hidden behind our bulkheads but within easy reach.

Literally at the last hour, this responsibility was shifted to the more senior crew of LCU-1654. The OINC was an E-8 master chief aboard the U.S.S. Spiegel Grove. It proved to be a mission that no one really wanted, and a successful outcome was the more important issue. This incident caused me to seriously reconsider my reenlistment possibilities. I had heard how RPGs (rocket-propelled grenades) had become a commonly used weapon in Lebanon's civil war. The precarious situation that a show of no force had presented played an important part in my decision to leave the Navy.

Soon after the evacuation of the U.S. citizens from Beirut, our responsibilities for the deployment of 1976 was lessened. We would be headed home soon. It was a very hopeful and joyous time for everyone. The expectancy of going home lightened all of my shipmate's hearts. We could write to our loved ones at home about our arrival in three or four weeks.

To my knowledge all of servicemen in the MARG 76 deployment received a letter in their military record from the joint chiefs of staff for a job well done. President Ford, Henry Kissinger, and the rest of America could breathe a sigh of relief that another conflict had been avoided.

Because of the Beirut crisis, our deployment had been extended a full month. It was hard to know when we would exactly arrive back at Little Creek. However, when we did arrive, I arranged for Cheryl to meet me in Atlanta as soon as it was possible.

Through our letter correspondence, over the length of the deployment I became exceedingly aware of our combined desire to return home to the Antioch community. That desire to return was etched deep into the souls of both Cheryl and me. I bounced our future ideas off BM1 Houston. In so many words he said I was a great professional but less of a sailor. That was a truly a bittersweet evaluation from a man I respected highly. As it referred to my family's future and my possible discharge, he added. "A man with your talent will leave the Navy and never look back."

Once again, as it had been after eighteen months in Guam, my faithful wife met me at the Atlanta airport. What a wonderful reunion it was. Both my family and hers joined in the day care of our two young children while Cheryl and I were in Atlanta. I had a burning desire to see Joe and a daughter I had never seen. On the day we arrived back in Watkinsville, Annie Jane Savage, a friend of the family, was keeping Susan. I shall never forget peering into the bassinet for the first time at our sleeping little angel. It was the summer of 1976.

My discharge was coming up again in March of 1977. Decisions had to be made, but they did not seem as pressing as when my first enlistment was up. Dad wanted very much for me to make a career out of the Navy. That decision, however, was not his to make. So I avoided that conversation when it came up. When the time drew closer, we started the preparation to leave the Navy and Little Creek but had no clue as to how we would make another start back home in Georgia.

Cheryl and I were happy when we called home with our final decision but sad when my Dad became angry about what we wanted to do. He had seen how successful Roger and Jimmie were in their respective branches of service and wanted that same security for our family. I squeezed out a few bitter tears after the telephone call, but nevertheless, our minds and hearts were set on going home.

On March 22, 1977, I went to the personnel department for Assault Craft Unit Two and received my DD-214 and honorable discharge. Uncle Sam moved our mobile home to a park within the city limits of Watkinsville. After we arrived back at home, I registered at the Department of Labor and started to draw unemployment until I could find a job. In my own way of thinking I wanted to change fields and try something different from communications.

# Fishing Patterns

The first few months back at home allowed me to slow down, take a deep breath, and scrutinize my way forward. For once in my life, if only for a short time, I was free to do this without fear of retaliation from a boss or peer, etc. Though my career as a civilian was just beginning, I was really quite relaxed about all of it. I found that my old love for fishing accomplished two things, a good supper and time to think.

If fishing were an exact science, it wouldn't be called fishing. Still, learning the best way to go about it is a virtue. Fish feed at certain times and strike impulsively. Putting all of this in a "nutshell" is why some people become professionals at it and others remain simply recreational fishermen.

Observing the weather and time of year when I had the most success fishing for different species of fish developed my fishing patterns. Similarly, these patterns developed also in hunting. Natural reproduction is at the center of good fishing and hunting patterns. The way different species of fish respond at spawning in the spring forms a pattern that can last a lifetime for the angler.

I discovered the natural freshwater species in the south, such as bluegill pan fish; crappie, white bass, largemouth bass, and catfish have different characteristics in their patterns for spawning. The pre-spawn period in February is best for crappie. Almost every year in Georgia, the cold days of February are tempered with ten days of warm springlike days. More times than not, these ten days come during the last two weeks of the month. Often these ten days will come in groups of two or three days at a time. Any avid angler can hardly resist casting his artificial bait a few times during these days.

White bass generally bites more frequently than the crappie in the early pre-spawn. Both species' natural willingness to strike at anything flashy usually results in catching several at a time. The intensity of the actions improves all through the spring until its close competitor in the food chain, the crappie, moves in on the action.

The largemouth bass becomes active in March and April. The bluegill starts to spawn in large beds in shallow water on the first full moon in May and continues this full moon pattern until September.

After the water has warmed up significantly after May, the catfish comes into focus. Since each of the freshwater species has its own curious characteristic, I discovered it was best for me to concentrate on which came first in the year and take them on one at a time since it required different tackle, live bait, and lures.

I bought a boat rack and purchased a small two-seat fiberglass eight-foot boat powered by a twelve-pound thrust trolling motor and twelve-volt battery. It was easy for me to load and unload it from the top of my Ford Pinto. I fished every small farm lake and pond in Oconee County where I was given permission. It was a quiet and stealthy little boat.

I netted my first trophy largemouth in Aunt Trudie's lake while fishing in this little boat. I bought several large spring lizards and made a lizard box for them. They were about six to nine inches in length and required a heavy-duty rod and line. My 1/0 hook was barely large enough to hook the lizard and leave the barb showing. I graduated from a spin caster reel to a bait caster.

A lady bass was fanning her spawning bed near some lily pads. I first located her by the wake in the shallow water and then by the top part of her tail fin fanning back and forth over the bed. She would swim away into deeper water and guard her bed from a short distance. When she moved off I cast and dropped the lizard right in the middle of her bed. It wasn't long before I saw the wake in the water as she moved in to investigate. My slack fishing line lay on top of the water. It began to curl away from her bed. I took up the slack in my line, and with one mighty jerk I set the hook in the corner of her mouth.

I was not anchored, so she took me for a ride. The drag on the rod and reel was set perfectly. With the exception of a slip every now and then, she pulled the boat and me around until she tired. She weighed seven and one-half pounds and was twenty-four inches long.

During the warming trend between the months of April and May, I would make the transition from crappie and bass fishing into the active bluegill pattern. This meant using lighter tackle and different bait. Though all freshwater fish will strike artificial lures, I have always had the tendency to use live bait. For bluegill I generally purchase 100-150 crickets and sink them in the water about eighteen inches below a pencil bobber with a number 8 Aberdeen hook.

One day after one such cast, I noticed my pencil bobber gliding across the water lying flat instead of vertical. My line curled with the increasing slack. With only eight-pound test line and a number 8 Aberdeen hook (a very small hook with a cricket as bait), I snagged an eight-pound lady bass. I tightened the drag on the line as much as I dared and started to back up the bank. There was a particular cluster of trash I was trying to avoid with my efforts. I barely guided her clear of the trash as she splashed around in ankle deep water. I reeled up the slack rapidly and put my thumb in her mouth and snatched my last trophy bass from the water. She was the largest I had ever caught, weighing just over eight pounds and twenty-six inches long.

During these few months of unemployment, it appeared to some that I was not concerned about landing a job. However I was trying to be faithful to the Lord by waiting upon his leading. I felt confident he had a plan for us. All I had to do was to recognize the open doors as he presented them. Until a door opened I was not concerned and enjoyed my freedom immensely.

There was no particular direction that I wanted to pursue. I knew I wanted something different from what I had done for eight years, or at least that is what I thought. I had not given much consideration to God's omniscience and how it would play an important role in my lifelong career. What lay before me was obviously unseen but very visible to the Lord. He knew what was best for me even if I did not.

# Norwood's Boy

The assistance from unemployment was not nearly enough to sustain the lifestyle we had become accustomed to. We did not have any bills, but the cost of living sank us financially. I started to lean on my own understanding when I should have paid more attention to the Lord's leading. I worked at odd jobs to supplement the meager unemployment checks. I had to report in weekly at the Department of Labor to keep the checks coming. I was also aware these checks could be sent through the mail.

One day after four months of unemployment, I stopped by the Department of Labor after a day of painting in Athens. I was wearing a pair of faded overalls spattered with paint. Some of that spatter was obviously in my hair and on my skin, but I was making good use of my time by stopping by the department while I was still in Athens. When I asked the lady behind the counter about being put on the mailing list for the checks, she made me feel about one foot tall. Her admonishment seemed harsh to me. She told me I was not trying hard enough to get a job and suggested fast food restaurants. She made it clear that I was not going to be put on the mailing list that day.

Feeling totally rejected, I stepped outside, looked up at the sky, and lifted up this short prayer. "What was that all about?"

The answer came back just as short and fast. "Look at yourself!"

I did, and I looked a mess. That was all the encouragement I needed. I decided to try a different approach.

The next week I dressed in my new three-piece suit that Mother had bought for me. I put my resume in a brief case and returned to the Department of Labor. I went to the same counter hoping the lady would not recognize me. With as much tact as I could muster,

I asked her about the possibilities of having my checks mailed to me instead of having to report in every week. She immediately addressed me as Mr. Lavender and invited me behind the counter to meet the person that could make that happen.

This time I stepped outside, lifted up my head, and thanked him. In that moment I was prompted to put in my application at Georgia Power. At the time I did not know their office was just down the street from the Department of Labor, so I went across town to the Georgia Power Operating Headquarters and asked if they were accepting applications. The receptionist sent me back across town to where I had just been and told me to ask for Clint Adams, the personnel manager.

With that little bit of information, I was directed upstairs to his office. His secretary's desk was located immediately after stepping from the elevator. I asked for Mr. Adams, and she straightway took me to him. After she introduced me to him, he seated me by his desk. On the corner of the desk, right in front of me, was a stack of Christian business cards. Right away I said, "I see you are a Christian too."

He was not only a Christian but a Gideon as well.

He scanned my resume and told me they were hiring technicians and that I might qualify. He also stated that the communications supervisor, Bill Christopher, was meeting with his boss as we spoke and asked would I like to meet them.

I said, "Of course."

Mr. Adams took me in to Norwood Donaldson's office. Seated by Norwood on the same side of his desk was Bill Christopher. After a proper introduction, the direction of their meeting took a turn. Everything seemed to be going right for me, but Bill did not like the interruption when Clint brought me in. Norwood scanned my resume also and told me he too had been a radioman in the Navy. We were familiar with the same kinds of equipment and spoke in detail about their features.

Georgia Power's parent company was the Southern Company. The smaller subsidiaries within the Southern Company were Georgia Power, Alabama Power, Mississippi Power, and Gulf Power. Starting about 1975, the parent company, Georgia Power, began building the largest privately owned telecommunication network in the world. That distinction did not last long since the information technologies revolution was just beginning. The process of hiring the technicians to build and maintain this network had begun.

The applicants for the job needed a two-year degree from a vocational technical school in communications and also hold a FCC license. Bill Christopher knew the demands of this high-tech field and wanted to be involved in the hiring of his technicians. With that being said, he had automatically eliminated me as a prospect.

However what his boss said at that end of our meeting I heard loud and clear. "The secret to what we can do for you is for you to get that license."

Though I had not planned it that way, I effectively had gone over Bill Christopher's head. For the interim period I would be answering directly to Norwood Donaldson.

It took a while for me to see God's hand in the orchestration of those events on that particular day. I had heard all through my active duty status that radiomen could do very well after military service if they could get their FCC license. I never thought I would ever be a willing candidate for that line of work.

In 1977 the starting salary for technician was just under $10,000. With the promise of an immediate raise to $11,500, I thought I owed it to my family to see what my chances were of landing the job. I drove to the Federal Communications Commission building in Atlanta, Georgia, to take the first of two tests for the license. That same day I obtained my third-class license on my background experience. Before leaving, the proctor asked me if I would like to take the second class test, which was the minimum requirement for the position I sought.

I was totally unprepared for what was inside that envelope. It may as well have been written in hieroglyphics. On one hand it was good that I saw what I was up against, but on the other hand I did not know that it counted as one of only two semiannual attempts allowed at the test.

Feeling satisfied with the day's accomplishments, I called Bill Christopher to let him know about my third class success. I asked him if he could hire me while I worked toward the second class. The answer was respectfully no. The Communications Department was already allowing one of his technicians to do that. He was a good technician but was having difficulty passing the second class exam.

My next question was, "Is everyone in Communications required to have a second class license?"

His answer was yes. Even the supervisors were required to have that level. Respectfully I asked Bill if everyone else that had successfully passed the second class test had retained all the electronic theory they had learned in vocational technical school.

There was a slight pause, as he said, "No. We had to take a refresher course."

I asked him where this was located and was surprised to find out that Elkins Institute was just two blocks from the FCC Building on Peachtree Street in Atlanta. Bill closed out our telephone conversation with, "I'm sorry, I cannot help you more, but at this point all I can do is encourage you."

Now I had a direction and a goal in mind, but I was still financially broke. I talked my chances over with my mom and dad and was so blessed when Dad gave me his Gulf credit card to pay for my trips to and from Elkins Institute. The pressure of possibly failing another critical test rushed in, and I became emotional as I accepted his card. "Dad, I may fail, this stuff is hard!"

He graciously brushed that comment away and gave me a hug. "You just take that card and pass that test."

The refresher course took eight weeks to complete. There had always seemed to be a professional void within me like something was missing. I found the next eight weeks of schooling exactly what I had been missing. I was not only intrigued with the instruction, but I enjoyed it as if I was putting a puzzle together. The hands on training that a student received at a vocational technical school was lacking but all the elements of electronic theory were put in order.

Some of the students were older professional men and women, but most were young men and women fresh out of tech school.

Within this field you find some really bright and gifted individuals. The instructors sought out these individuals and sent them to be tested after about five weeks of instruction. If they were successful, they were expected to bring back to Elkins Institute any questions on the test that had not been covered in school. As a result, the testing procedure at Elkins simulated the actual test that provided the license. Elkins Institute sent me to be tested at the FCC after the sixth week. There were a hundred questions to answer on the examination. There were four multiple-choice answers from which to select the correct answer. A passing grade 75 was expected. When the proctor graded my second attempt at the second class, I scored a 71. I was not discouraged since I had two more weeks of school. My unemployment benefits were running out about the same time.

The next week I waited in line with all the other testing prospects. I received the shock of a lifetime when the proctor told me I could not take the test for another six months. A wave of practicality came over me. "Mam!" "Most of these young folks don't even know what they are going to do with their lives. I have a wife, two children, and a job waiting on me if I pass this test!"

She responded. "Would you like to speak to the director of the FCC and ask for a waiver?"

I said, "Yes mam!"

She took me to see Mr. Ditty. Having given it a trial run with the proctor, I repeated my plight. Mr. Ditty responded. "If you bring me a letter from your prospective employer stating what you have just told me, I will waiver you."

I thanked him and rushed back to Athens to speak to Norwood.

It was getting late in the day when I arrived at Norwood's office. I was still feeling the pressure as I invited myself into his office. He finished up what he was doing in silence as I unloaded my situation on top of him. Still silent he reached for a scrap piece of paper and began to write.

As he handed me the paper, he spoke for the first time. "Will that do?"

Hurriedly I scanned over the note and replied, "Yes, sir!" and headed for the exit.

He stopped me at the door and said, "Have my secretary type that up on a Georgia Power Company letter head."

The next day I reported directly to Mr. Ditty. When he read the letter Norwood had written, he told me to show it to the proctor and I would be waivered.

I let out a big sigh and responded to his graciousness. "Mr. Ditty, I can't take that test today. I've got to study. This is my last chance."

He understood and said to show the letter when I was ready.

I purchased a pack of 3x5 index cards and begin to write on them the thirty-three electronic formulas I had learned at Elkins. On one side was a question that would cause me to give the associated answer. With a little preparation, I showed Cheryl how to test my knowledge of these formulas. We burned the midnight oil that night, and after a pot of coffee I went back to Atlanta the next morning.

The first order of business for the proctors was to clear all the calculators and seat the students. I went to the back right rear corner and sat in the last desk purposely. Previously my experience had been that the faster students would bump my desk as they walked by. This was very annoying and interrupted my train of thought.

Before I opened the envelope, I began to make a formula sheet from memory. Of the thirty-three possible electronic formulas to use for the test, I remembered twenty-six. I opened the envelope and began my last chance at receiving the FCC license. I worked the easiest questions first. After going through the one hundred questions, I knew that I had answered sixty-six correctly. I went through them again answering the second hardest questions. That time through I answered another ten correctly. My score was at seventy-six but that wasn't good enough for me. The third time through I painstakingly worked most of the remaining twenty-four questions. I could not be as sure about the answers on those questions but felt confident that I had answered at least twelve of them correctly and made an educated guess on half of the remaining twelve. I was the last one to leave the room that day out of about fifty students.

The proctor placed an overlay answer sheet on top of my test, and in about fifteen seconds she said, "You passed."

I felt as if I was floating on air for the rest of the day.

I wanted to surprise Cheryl with the news. She was not home when I came in, but she could walk almost anywhere in Watkinsville and still not be more than twenty minutes away. I sat down and devised a scheme. I tried looking as sad as I could when she came in. I said not a word, so she would ask how I had done on the test. I tried to fool her by saying I had not passed. I must not have been a very good liar. She saw something in my expression and ran across the room, jumped straddle of me, grabbed me by the collar, and started shaking me and shouting. "Let's go to Georgia Power right now!"

It was about 4:25, and they closed at 5 p.m., but we went to Georgia Power. Cheryl and I stepped off the elevator, and less than three steps away stood Clint Adams and Norwood Donaldson. I showed my verification card, first to Norwood, and then he passed it to Clint and said as he tapped me on the chest with the back of his hand, "This is my man. Hire him."

I found out from my peers after I had started to work that Bill Christopher had derisively referred to me as Norwood's boy. Nevertheless, after working the next seven years for him, he promoted me three times to senior technician, and my salary quadrupled. I cannot take credit for that success for I believe it was a blessing from God. Bill Christopher was also a fine Christian man and a great supervisor. He was one of the best superiors I ever had in the field of information technology. He was one of very few immediate supervisors I had in my forty-three-year career.

Before I started to work, I had another meeting with Clint Adams, the personnel manager. We were discussing payroll deductions when the monthly deduction of $120 for a medical insurance plan came to the forefront. As broke as Cheryl and I had become, 10 percent of my monthly income seemed like too much to pay for insurance. Thanks to Mr. Adams he drove a hard bargain on that insurance deduction. Though I had a choice, it would have been a dreadful mistake in retrospect not to have it in place. He encouraged me to get used to the fact that the plan was designed to have my best interests at the center of it and I would not miss it after a few raises in pay.

How honest and true was everything he conveyed to me that day. Fifteen years later I saw how important $7.90 of that $120 was for the rest of my life. That small amount was the monthly payment for long-term disability.

# The Seven-Year Plan

After my honorable discharge from the Navy, Cheryl and I set forth with a plan for our American dream. Since our work had been committed to the Lord, we also realized that seven represented his number of completeness. Within those parameters, we put together a seven-year plan to purchase land and build a house on it.

By the end of 1977 I had become an ordained deacon at Antioch Christian Church. On a beautiful Sunday afternoon after church, we were on our way home to our mobile home in Watkinsville about seven miles away. About three and a half miles up the road, we decided to cut off on Oliver Bridge Road. It was unpaved and had only a few old homes along its two and a half-mile length.

James Marshall, a local real estate man, had several signs posted on both sides of Oliver Bridge Road with land for sale. The property on both sides of the road was filled with timber and woodlands. We were still in our casual Sunday attire. It was a pretty tough hike for both of us through the briars and honeysuckle to the property markers. We were not excited about the first five-acre tract we looked at. We were happy to get back to the road where the car was parked. We then decided to look on the other side of the road up a moderately steep hill with a mixture of pines and hardwoods.

The climb up to the top of the hill was pretty tough, but when we reached the crest a welcomed breeze rustled through the hardwood leaves. The visibility was better than what both Cheryl and I had expected. We immediately felt at home. We wanted to buy the whole hill. To purchase the hill would require buying 13.6 acres. From the top of the hill, we did not know the hill had been surveyed into two tracts. One was surveyed to contain 8.6 acres, and on the other side of the hill was the additional five-acre lot. James

Marshall was eager to sell, but he was concerned the bank might not approve our loan for both of the lots. After prayerful consideration, we applied for a loan of $6,500 for the 8.6-acre lot. The loan was approved, and we began preparation to move our mobile home to our new address.

The Georgia Power Company hired me as a salary, nonunion personnel. I was assigned a vehicle and worked a forty-hour week from 8:00 a.m. to 5:00 p.m. After hours I worked on the property. The first order of business was to cut through the woods from the Oliver Bridge Road to provide a right of way for our driveway. The driveway also created a lane for the Walton Electric Membership Corporation to provide power to the top of the hill.

I purchased a chainsaw and began to cut down the trees. I cut them into firewood lengths and stacked multiple cords on each side of the unfinished driveway. Once I had blazed my way to the top of the hill, I began to cut out enough space for a tractor-trailer to maneuver our mobile home into place among the hardwoods.

Next I contacted James Elder, the bulldozer operator. James Elder was always the man to hire for that kind of work. For a day's worth of work, Mr. Elder graded the driveway and a lot for our mobile home.

Next I called the well drillers. They started boring on top of the hill, but just beneath the surface of the ground was solid rock. After boring into solid rock for about twenty-five feet the well drillers pulled up and selected a spot beside the driveway and hit twelve foot of water relatively easy. Then they dug a trench from the well to the top of the hill for the main waterline and buried an electrical cable to power the pump.

Excavation for the septic tank and field lines came next. We invested most of my first nine months income into land improvements.

Walton EMC connected to our temporary service pole, and we were ready to move by April of 1978. There are a few "red letter" moments that are etched into one's memory for a lifetime. Such a moment was the morning Dad came to visit the spot we were planning to live. As I write, I am as old now as my dad was then. The lane up the hill had been graded. No one had driven on the driveway at that time. We met Dad at the bottom of the hill. Joe and Susan were with us and ran up the hill as best as super toddlers could run just in front of us.

Dad spoke with sheer satisfaction. "God bless them. Their little lives are just now opening up."

As we continued on our upward hike, he made another complimentary and satisfying remark. "You have that firewood stacked like candy."

It was a time of celebration for our friends and us. Having made a successful transition from the Navy to finding a good job, purchasing land and living on it within one year were a big step.

The area we had cleared for the mobile home to be parked was about 150 yards from the main road in the middle of our woods. We threw a yard party for all the friends and neighbors. Wood was within easy reach, and we kept a fire going for hours at the time. There was always venison to grill, and we competed in horseshoe tournaments by the large fire and lantern light. If there were not enough chairs for everyone to have a seat, they simply rolled over a large piece of firewood that had not been split. It was a rugged start, but most of our friends were still in their twenties, and it was all part of the fun.

Spirit and Dad, May 14, 1972

Misty Blue, 1979

Cheryl and Red, December 13, 1986

# Misty Blue

Once a friend said to me, "You and Cheryl have always had horses, haven't you?"

I had never really thought about that, but it was true. I knew Cheryl loved horses enough that she traded her bedroom suit to her brother if he would buy her one. Spirit came into our lives before we were even married. Dad and Mom allowed Spirit to pasture with our cows while I was in Guam. He was about thirteen hands and more of a large pony than a horse. Spirit spent the rest of his life on Dad's farm before he became founded and was put down in 1978. Now that we had our own property I made a corral from long slender oaks and bought a registered quarter horse from Mr. Thompson, a local horse rancher.

It was a premature move to purchase a registered quarter horse since we had no fence, and the children took up most of our time and responsibility. But I wanted Cheryl to have the real thing.

Mr. Thomason's stud was called "The Hancock Stallion." He was a beautiful white and gray speckled roan stud. I rode him once. That was enough. Mr. Thomason's boys were the same age as we were. On occasions we would ride their horses. When I became interested in purchasing a filly from the stallion's bloodline, Mike Thomason allowed me to ride The Hancock Stallion. I knew very little about how to use the reins on a trained horse, especially a stud.

I had barely swung myself into the saddle when we were off at a full gallop. It was all I could do to hold on to the saddle horn. I knew I was not in control and moving much faster than I wanted to go. A half-mile from where I had mounted, the stallion ran into a wooded area. He jumped over an open well. The saddle had slipped to one side, and I looked down for a place to land. I held on tightly as the stud jumped over the opened well. The undergrowth slowed the horse to a walk. I thought that was a good idea and dismounted. We walked back to the barn. Horses are good people trainers, if you let them.

We selected a six-month-old filly and named her Misty Blue. She was a blue roan daughter of The Hancock Stallion. At that age she was basically black with a white star on her forehead. All through her coat were white hairs that gave the appearance of glistening sequins. She was a beautiful and sweet-natured horse. I was told when she became a mature horse she would be solid white.

I became Misty Blue's trainer. Before I built a corral, I built a small shed/stable about eight feet by ten feet high. That is where she stayed most of the time until I finished the corral. I broke her to the halter and was able to pet, curry her, lift her feet, and stake her out to graze. Misty Blue needed more experience before Cheryl could handle her. Keeping her fed, groomed, and growing was an important job. I was pleased with her progress, and she seemed to trust me more each day as she grew.

Ponies and horses are measured in hands, which represents four inches. Ponies are less than fourteen and one-half hands high at the withers. To be considered a horse the height ranges from fourteen and one-half hands upward to seventeen and one-half hands and beyond. Quarter horses were crossbred from the Spanish mustang and thoroughbreds to produce a horse with stamina and speed for working cattle. Within a quarter of a mile, the quarter horse is faster, but the thoroughbred can maintain a paced canter for distances beyond. Misty Blues height was fourteen and one-half hands.

I borrowed an old saddle to begin that part of her training. When she became accustomed to all the horse tack necessary for riding, it was time to mount her. That was a big step for her and me. I walked her to my neighbor's pasture and gave it a try. She took the bit relatively easy. I did not want to be harsh on the reins and hurt her mouth. It was a thin line in finding the right pressure. She immediately went into a fast canter/gallop. That was OK with me so long as I could stay on her back. I figured she would slow down eventually, and we could call it enough for one day. Suddenly at a quarter of a mile, the saddle started to loosen and slipped. I hit the ground rolling. Lesson number one—always start with a good saddle that fits the rider. Though it was an abrupt ending, to that phase I was still very pleased with Misty Blue's progress.

The makeshift corral from the slender oaks did not last very long. When the wind blew, the trees moved. The slender oaks were nailed to the moving trees. The rails eventually worked loose and Misty Blue got out. I was working overtime on an important job and could not come home. Cheryl called me to tell me she was out. I convinced Cheryl that she was halterbroke and for her to get a lead rope snapped to her halter and tie her up until I could get home.

Sometime after midnight I arrived back at our mobile home. Misty Blue was so beautiful, tied under the security light at a nearby tree. She whinnied at me as I arrived at the doorstep and immediately came over and put her chin on my shoulder. Everything seemed so peaceful and safe. Lesson number two—when tying up a horse, always tie them up short with no slack.

I was fatigued and went to bed. Our dogs began to bark incessantly right after I dropped off to sleep. What I saw next is too horrible to write about. The dogs had caused her to wrap the slack in the long lead rope around one of her back legs tightly against the tree, and she had fallen. The bone was working free outside of her stationary hoof that was wrapped against the tree. I straightway retrieved my deer rifle and wept the rest of the night.

I called in and took a personal day off. I did not allow Cheryl to look outside until the County Road department had come to bury our beautiful horse along with our misery.

# Twenty-One Percent Interest Rates

The new mobile home that we purchased in Virginia was a 1976 model. It had two bedrooms, a full bath and utility space, a living room, and a kitchen. By 1980 we had literally outgrown it. Joe and Susan's small bedroom was furnished with a bunk bed, but at the ages of six and four we could see the inevitable approaching. They would soon need their own space.

Soon after moving on to the property, I started to study the interest rates for a construction loan. It seemed that every time I inquired about the rates, they had increased by one or two percentage points. I became more and more discouraged with each increase. In 1979, 10 percent was tolerable.

Cheryl and I studied a magazine dedicated exclusively to house plans. We settled on a ranch-style house with a basement. The interior heated space was 1,733 square feet. We ordered the complete house plans for our home. Its dimensions were approximately thirty feet by sixty feet with three bedrooms, two full baths, a hallway, a large family room, a breakfast room, kitchen, dining room, a living room, and a foyer. The plans were the very first step, and it turned out to be a good investment.

By the time we ordered and received the plans, the interest rates had moved to 12 percent. The lending institutions at the time would only finance 80 percent, and we had to come up with 20 percent. That slowed our plans as we figured out how we could come up with 20 percent. The 8.6 acres was worth a portion of that percentage, but we still owed most of the $6,500. I asked James Marshall how much he would charge to build the house. One look at our plans, and he gave us the rough estimate of $87,000. Our portion of that was about $17,500. That was no small amount. We would have to apply for nearly $70,000. The figures seemed to be insurmountable.

By the end of 1979 the interest rates on new construction loans had started to rise astronomically. I remember seriously considering a construction loan at 18 percent but thought better of it.

In a rebellious approach I started to implement the same practices that brought about our purchase of the land and our move to live on it. It had taken much of my own involvement to improve the land to the point of livability. In so doing I had utilized my own resources and created enough equity for it to be appraised in dollars and cents.

I did not know how far I could go into the construction of our house, but I figured if I built it exactly according to the plans, the same equitable result would count as the 20 percent collateral we needed.

I stapled the pages of our house plans to the walls of our bedroom in the mobile home. The last thing I saw at night before falling asleep and the first thing I saw when morning came was another phase of work that needed to be accomplished. I began to fall back on what my dad had taught me as a teenager.

In close proximity to our mobile home, about three feet, I began the grading. My dad had taught me how to start with batter boards, pull lines, and line levels. Just outside the corners of where our house would sit, I drove three sharp stakes and nailed two level boards to it on all four corners. I set up Dad's transit in the middle of where our home would sit and calculated where the pull lines had to be suspended to form a *level pad*. Because of so much rock beneath the surface, I decided to forego the basement space. It would require added cost to blast and remove all the rock. Before I pulled the lines, I removed a few more trees.

To move heavy equipment like a bulldozer, it requires a job at least one to three days in length. I called Mr. James Elder, the bulldozer operator, and asked him for another day's worth of work. He worked most of the day pushing up the stumps and shaping the grade within the batter boards. Toward the end of the day, he shut down the dozer and presented me with his work on the grade. I told him he wasn't finished yet. He seemed surprised. I immediately put the pull lines back up and pulled one across the grade showing him how much more dirt was needed. He did not trust my calculation, so I quickly set up the transit and spun it around the dimensions of the grade. He still did not trust the way I was presenting my case, so he went home and retrieved his own transit and set it up by the one I had borrowed from Dad. I was not worried for I knew he would have to relent in the end.

When he looked through his transit and then mine, all he could say was, "Where am I going to get that much dirt?"

That was an easy answer for me. Standing on top of our hill, I waved my hand over our property and said, "You have eight and one-half acres, help yourself."

He returned the next day and worked all day. Once he had got the mental picture of what I wanted and could trust the lines, he did a fantastic job.

He was so happy with his work he brought his son down to see it and proudly said to him, "That is how you steal dirt."

I needed the grade to be level because of the contiguous stages of the floor plans. I needed my calculations to be perfect so when I put in an order for work and materials, there would be no embarrassing surprises.

I had not yet applied for a building permit. I was working privately on my own property and using my own funds, so I did not see the need at that point.

The footing for the foundation required that a ditch be dug beneath the surface at least eighteen inches deep. Inside the ditch I was required to drench the soil with a thirty-year termite deterrent. I did so and saved the label from the highly expensive and highly toxic solution for proof of treatment to the loan officers.

On top of the footing soil I bought enough steel reenforced rebar to go around the periphery and covered it with concrete footing. I ordered enough regular cinder blocks for the circumference of our house. I bought mortar mix and began to lay the blocks. I left one end of the foundation open and free of blocks so I could order gravel to place on top of the 1733 square foot vapor barrier (a polyethylene sheet on top of the soil beneath the gravel). I figured the cubic yards of gravel needed to provide exactly four inches across the grade.

I ordered two dump truck loads of gravel from L. C. Curtis and Sons, a mining operation just down the highway. The huge dump trucks backed carefully into the grade and dumped small piles along the length of the foundation. It was exactly the right amount as I leveled the small piles into an even four inches across the grade. The next phase of the foundation required the plumbing plans.

Stubbing the plumbing in the exact place on a concrete pad has to be perfect. It was the most challenging part of the construction. I purchased four-inch PVC sewer pipe and some two-inch drainage PVC and of course cold and hot water supply lines. Using the same method with pull lines, I calculated the exact spots to turn up the standpipes for each application. I measured and figured on this phase extensively.

The four inches of gravel made the plumbing easier. I was able to rake away the gravel and make the pipes slightly stationary at the correct placement before raking the gravel back over the pipes and making them more secure.

I finished laying the cinder blocks on the open end of the foundation. Next came the form blocks. They were a cutaway version of the cinder block, allowing the concrete to flow to the outer extremities of the dimensions.

As I had done with the gravel, I figured the exact amount of cubic yards of concrete four inches thick needed to make the pad.

My most satisfying moment of the foundation construction came when the last truck of concrete had a small amount left after the pad had been poured. It was about 5:00 p.m. and time for everyone to shut down and go home.

The truck operator asked me. "Where do you want me to dump this small amount I have left?"

I asked him how much he had. I did not want it dumped in the yard and thus become an eyesore. He estimated it was a couple of wheelbarrows full. The two of us began to brainstorm. Brilliantly the operator asked where our outside air conditioning and heat pump unit was going to sit. The light bulb went off in my head, and I asked his indulgence for about five more minutes as I hurriedly built a crude form from scrap lumber lying nearby.

The truck had not moved from where it had finished pouring the pad. He dumped every last piece of graveled concrete into the crude form and helped me work a board over the top of it to make it level. It had been another perfect calculation with help from my Invisible Friend. It was the first time I had given any thought at all to the outside air and heating unit. I gave thanks to the Lord.

In 1980 I again checked with bank about getting a construction loan. I could not believe my ears. It had gone up to 21.46 percent. To me it presented a closed door. My blood pressure soared upward with the absurdity of the rising rates.

I was driving my company van back from Technology Park in Norcross, Georgia, with maintenance parts to repair the microwave network. I became very uneasy physically. Pain began to shoot down my left arm. I pulled over and began to walk around the vehicle to try and shake it off, but it only got worse. I reversed my way of thinking and thought I had better lay down. My old nemesis was back, and it had taken control. It had been exactly ten years since my last attack in Guam. I laid down in the van and gave it prayerful consideration. Reluctantly I picked up the microphone of my radio and called in for help. Bill Christopher asked me if I could hold on until he could send a couple of my peers to pick up the van and drive me to the doctor's office. I told him I could but to send them quickly. I was about thirty-five minutes from Athens.

One of my fellow peers, Randy Kittle, drove my van while I remained reclined in the back. About an hour and ten minutes after it had begun, we were at Dr. Tallmadge's office. I had loosened my shirt and taken off my shoes seeking comfort, having no luck in that matter. Randy parked the van and waited. Rudely I walked through the waiting room with my shoes in my hands and sought Dr. Tallmadge. I was interrupting, but I felt I had a good reason.

When he looked at me with a scornful face, I simply said, "Doc, you had better take a look at me!"

He had the nurse seat me in a room and straightway came to me. He asked a few short questions, and I panted the answers as he tightened the blood pressure cup. He cut the circulation completely off in my left arm and he began to listen.

I said, "Dr. Tallmadge, you're cutting my circulation off!"

He replied harshly. "Shut up! I know it!"

For at least two minutes he listened to my heart in silence with his eyes closed.

He loosened the cup and explained. "I don't think there has been any damage. However I am sending you to the emergency room with instructions. Because of my age I can't work in the hospital system anymore, but I can communicate to the doctors what I have discovered. When you arrive, they will be waiting for you. Your blood pressure is extremely high, 180/110, and your heart rhythm is rapid and irregular. When they release you, call my office, and I will talk with you."

Randy took me to the emergency room and returned to work.

Four hours later I was released from the ER and I called Dr. Tallmadge. He had called in a prescription for me and gave me a follow-up appointment. At the follow-up appointment Dr. Tallmadge put all the cards on the table. His diagnosis was proximal auricular tachycardia. I told him I had it happen ten years prior to this incident in Guam. He said he had that condition himself along with fifty of his patients. He explained as best as he could the electrophysiological nature of the condition.

When I asked him how the condition affected longevity of life, he said, to his knowledge, it did not affect longevity.

When I asked him how old were the fifty patients with our condition, he paused before he answered. "I'll admit you are the youngest."

I was thirty years old. Dr. Tallmadge was almost eighty.

He adjusted my prescription and added another medication.

When I asked how long I would have to take them he said, "For the rest of your life."

It was a shocking revelation. Except for this condition I was a specimen of good health. I was six feet one inch tall weighed 225 pounds. I was strong as an ox. In self-pity I went home and wept over this chink in my physical armor.

Unbeknownst to the doctors and me, this was the beginning of a spiral downward to places few men have been or would have to go.

In 1980 changes were being made in the way the doctors and insurance companies provided care. There was a specialist in almost every medical field. Patients were required to have a primary care physician who would act as a liaison sending the patients in the proper direction if they had special needs. Dr. Tallmadge retired soon after my second attack and some time passed before I acquired a new primary care physician. Dr. Dubose had taken some of Dr. Tallmadge's patients, and he was the doctor I was seeing to get my prescriptions filled. Dr. Tallmadge and I had tried all the medications that were helping to keep my heart stable. With each appointment, Dr. Dubose started over with all the same medications in an effort to help my condition. I knew we were backing up with that approach; however, I remained patient and followed his direction. Instead of improving, the return to the old drugs revealed how desperate my situation had become.

On my last visit to Dr. Dubose's office, he asked me if I would like to see a cardiologist. I said sure, if he thought I needed to see one. He called the Athens Cardiology Group to set up an appointment. I waited to get the time of the appointment and listened in on the conversation.

When the receptionist at Athens Cardiology Group set an appointment date two months away, Dr. Dubose became indignant. He said, "Listen! This man has a serious heart condition and needs to be seen right away!"

The next day Dr. James Miller of the Athens Cardiology Group became my cardiologist.

I took with me to Athens Cardiology the recent medical history since the last attack, and they changed the medications to the best known at the time for my condition. I was scheduled for periodic appointments every three months and returned to work.

I was promoted to senior technician after five years with the company. I continued to work hard at whatever job I was assigned.

The job requirements of a senior technician working within the Southern Company Telecommunications Network demanded proficiency in telephone key systems, telephone exchanges, cabling, digital data transmission, microwave radio infrastructure, multiplex channelization, mobile radio field repair, mobile radio installation, professionally driving many miles, tower maintenance, and maintaining 100 percent redundant systems including backup generators for remote sites and local offices. Anything and everything necessary to efficiently run a complete telecommunication network was the responsibility of the early IT technicians. Some ditch digging, cable installation, and mobile radio installation may have been the most laborious of my chores. Often I would start early in the morning on an installation assignment and be ringing wet with sweat by 10:00 a.m. Simply listed, all these responsibilities do not explain the complexity and interworking of each requirement. Learning color codes and properly installing twenty-five to two hundred pair cables and associated circuitry were expected.

Our department was divided into two primary parts. One was installation, and the other was maintenance though it quite often overlapped. Georgia Power, Alabama Power, Mississippi Power, Gulf Power, and Duke Power had their individual regions within them. Georgia Power was divided into four regions. Each region had a primary headquarters. Ours was in Athens, Georgia, and we dispersed from there each workday. Our northeastern region IT department had Bill Christopher as its superintendent, his secretary, and two supervisors, and then it was the rest of us totaling ten. All but the secretary had assigned vehicles.

As a fringe benefit, all senior technicians were allowed to order the type of vehicle that best suited them for their particular function. Bill asked me into his office to discuss the vehicle I wanted to order. My job required that I maintain our remote microwave sites. This meant that I quite often drove in rough terrain up mountains where the tower and sites were located. I did not feel guilty at all when I put in my order for a 302 cubic inch V-8, 4×4 fuel-injected Ford Bronco. I of course had it loaded with air conditioning AM/FM radio, inside locking hubs, and power windows. The company also had the cargo space loaded with $50,000 worth of high-tech test equipment and all my professional tools. We were on call twenty-four hours a day and were allowed to drive our vehicles home but were expected to dispatch from home to anywhere in the region at any time of the day or night.

# The Construction Loan

After President Reagan was sworn into office in January of 1981, the interest rates for new home construction loans began to drop. On the bright side of the ridiculously high interest rates was how it had motivated me to drive my own bargain to accomplish the end result of our seven-year plan. The foundation for our house was completed and paid in full. I did not know how much in dollars and cents the total job was worth, but I figured it might pass for our 20 percent collateral.

I continued with that approach. The slowdown in new home construction because of the high interest rates had put the construction workers out of work. The boom in new construction seemed inevitable if the rates kept dropping. Before they were hired back, I sought out some of these workers. I was mainly interested in those construction workers that did phases of work that I was not proficient in doing. My approach was to do as much by myself as possible but yield to the professionals on the phases I was not familiar with accomplishing in a timely manner. Construction loans were generally paid out in installments over a six-month period after each phase of construction was completed.

The next phase of construction was the framing. I had met a framer through the Oconee County Church Soft Ball League and bumped into him at the grocery store. I asked him if he was obligated to his construction company or free to frame up our house. He said he would be happy to do our framing. He gave me his cost per foot, and it totaled $1,700. All I had to do was furnish the lumber and material to keep him and his crew working.

I started immediately to seek out each professional that I needed to complete the construction in six months. On three sheets of paper

# IT CAN'T BE LUCK

I began to list the name, address, and contact number for each professional. In the two columns beside the name, I listed labor cost and material cost. For labor cost of the phases that I could do, I simply put a 0 and listed the material cost. When I had finished the three-page columned outline, the total for our construction loan came to $28,500. That was quite a different figure from $87,000.

The day the interest rate hit 12.75 percent on the way down; I took out my sheet and called the professionals on the list to confirm their estimated cost with them. The next day I went to the bank to fill out the application for our construction loan. The process started with the local branch vice president. It mushroomed to six other vice presidents at the main office. With each appointment, I carried my three sheets of columned outline. They were extremely skeptical that I could build the house for that amount.

My reply was, "With the work I have already done and unless these folks lied to me on the phone last night and unless I am lying to you about what else I can do, I don't see why I can't build it for that much."

Ultimately their answer came. "You have certainly done your homework, but let's add $5,000 to that figure for good measure."

The loan was approved, and I began to spend money like a millionaire, within budget of course. I left for work one morning, and when I returned home the framing was reaching the sky. Within a day or two I made my first draw on the loan and gladly paid off the framer, but not before his contractor called me inquiring about my motives. I had to remind him of the free enterprise system in America and reassured him he could rehire his framer when I was finished with him.

With each phase and each draw, the house was nearing completion. The transition from the mobile home into the house was easy but not necessarily smooth. We sold the mobile home to a lady that wanted to put it on Lake Oconee, and we agreed upon a date. That meant no matter how close to completion we were, I had to make the new house habitable and have the bare necessities bought so I could install them. I installed a surface unit and sink, completed one bathroom, etc. We had appliances stacked in the middle of the large family room while we were still staining and painting. We finished our home on time and under budget at the end of our seven-year plan. I made the last draw on the loan, and our first mortgage was $33,500. In the breakfast room we hung our motto. "As for me and my house we will serve the Lord" (Joshua 24:15).

Before the children started going to school, Cheryl stayed at home providing the necessary care children at that age need. Several companies employed Cheryl after that. She worked at Reliance Electric before we married. After we married, she worked at Blue Cross and Blue Shield, Georgia Custom Designs, and Thaxton Turkeys before settling into a career of accounting at the University of Georgia Press. She attended Athens Vocational Technical School and finished their prescribed courses in accounting. Once the University System of Georgia employed her, she was never turned down for any position she applied for within their system. She presently is employed by the College of Education at the University of Georgia as a business manager.

While we were in the Navy, we had bought a new Mazda RX3 Sedan. We traded it when the children came to a newer RX3 Station Wagon. The rotary engines wore out, and we had become a two-car family soon after we were discharged from the Navy. After the two Mazda, our automobiles were always used vehicles. Cheryl was driving a sporty five-speed Plymouth Sapporo, and I was driving a Ford Pinto. The benefit of driving a company vehicle did not exempt me from needing my own personal vehicle for non-company work and recreation. I bought a boat rack to haul my small fishing boat around on top of the Pinto. For short distances, I even hauled the deer I harvested on the hood and sometimes in the boot.

By 1984 with the income from both of us, we were able to afford some things we needed and a few things we did not need but wanted. I made prior arrangements at the Georgia Power Credit Union and started my search for a new truck. In Commerce, Georgia, on my lunch hour, I looked at a 1984 Ford, 4x4, V-8 custom-style side pickup. I liked it and told the dealer I would be coming back through Commerce around 5:00 p.m. I told him I wasn't one for dickering and for him to give me his absolute best price and work it up. If I liked it I would sign. If I thought it was too much, I would continue looking.

I thought $11,500 was a fair price and made arrangements to pick up the check at the credit union. The next Saturday morning, I was driving my very first new pickup home. I kept it for twenty-five years. By the time I had owned it ten years I had put more in fuel cost than what it cost brand new.

1985

On Lake Oconee

1985 on Lake Oconee

# The Spiral Downward

Between 1984 and 1994, my heart condition manifests itself after shorter periods of lying almost dormant. In Guam at age twenty and in Athens, Georgia, at age thirty, its manifestation was the same, high blood pressure with a rapid pulse. This was the most evident symptom, but having the condition occur in the presence of a doctor was next to impossible. Only when it lingered long enough for the doctors to see it were they able to accurately diagnose and treat me. The medications kept it under control most of the time. However, as it was with the transition from the primary care physicians to the cardiologist, the transition from one stage to the next brought new terminology and technology.

By 1985 I had been under the care of the Athens Cardiology Group for five years. At this juncture the changes I would undergo were all new territory for me. The condition worsened, and the medications strengthened. The attacks came more frequently, but I had learned to find a quiet place and lie still and horizontal until my heart reverted back to a normal rhythm. Dr. Miller asked me if I had a job where I could take a "siesta" at noon. I told him about my travel time, and by noon I was often at a remote microwave facility in a climate-controlled room and I said, "Yes, I could take a siesta."

Dr. Miller said if I even dozed for a moment, it would be a benefit to me. So, under the doctor's orders I put a short siesta into practice on my lunch hours whenever possible.

Incredibly, the condition slowly took control. I began to utilize my vacation instead of my ten days of annual sick leave. It was hard to discuss with anyone what I was feeling. I was not resting well at night, and I was more fatigued during the day.

At age thirty-five, I began to notice an increase in my weight from 225 pounds to 235. It was very difficult for me to maintain a weight below 235 pounds. One of my peers, Robert Saine, and I were about the same statue, and he too noticed an increase in his weight, so I thought it was natural. We often held each other accountable on the storeroom scales at the operating headquarters. However, my weight increased upward to 252. Often, my clothing would be drenched from a heavy sweat, but curiously I felt better afterward. This became a way of life for me for the next few years.

I bought a nice eighteen-foot Pro Craft fishing boat with a 150-horse power Mercury Black Max outboard motor. It was a jewel. Ironically the day I brought the boat home Cheryl had delivered to our home a new filly from a horse sale at the university. What could I say? I got my boat, and she got her horse, end of discussion. We had some fun times making trips to Lake Oconee on picnics, swimming, and fishing trips. We pulled inner tubes for the kids, and we had a ball. There is a reason I bring the boat into the picture. While floating around the boat with our life jackets on, I noticed for the first time a wheezing when I breathed. I first thought I was catching a chest congestion from riding in our air-conditioned vehicles while wearing wet clothes. I did not sleep well at all that night and called in sick on Monday. That happened often. I had used up my ten days sick leave and started to use my vacation days.

My mother was surprised, at times, to find me home and inquired about every little detail. She later talked with my dad saying, "I'm worried about Billy. Something is not right with him." Truer words were never spoken.

Twenty years after my first attack in 1990, I experienced an added symptom to my condition. In 1989 while on the job in Elberton, Georgia, the initial symptoms reoccurred, and nothing I seemed to do gave me any relief. I became concerned. I was forty-five minutes from Athens. I called in to my supervisor and told him I needed to see a doctor. He offered to send a driver for me and asked if I needed assistance. I told him I would be OK. It would work smoother if I simply drove back and went straight to the doctor.

Because of the change in the availability of cardiologist, I needed to be referred by my primary care physician. Since Dr. Tallmadge had retired and Dr. Dubose had already hooked me up with Athens Cardiology, I was a little confused as to which doctor to see. Med Trends was an immediate care facility, and a person could be seen without an appointment and without an emergency room visit. I went straight to Med Trends for the first time. Dr. Jones saw me after a short waiting period.

After listening through his stethoscope, he asked me. "Do you know you have a heart condition?"

I said, "Yes."

He asked. "Do you have a cardiologist?"

I answered, "Yes."

He said, "You need to go back to see him."

With that he gave me six Lasix tablets from his office supply, and that was the extent of my visit. No one told me what else he wrote in my new file.

I took my first Lasix tablet ever. Within four hours I started to urinate frequently, and with each trip to the restroom, I felt better. The pills worked so wonderfully I saw no need to take another approach and saved the remaining five for when I really needed them. That night and the subsequent two or three nights, I rested much better. After about four days, I began to feel bloated once again and took my second pill. Just as before I was soon feeling and resting much better, the inevitable was approaching.

After three weeks I had ran out of the pills, so I returned to Med Trends.

I had just settled into my seat after checking in when Dr. Jones' attentive nurse shouted my name across the waiting room. "Mr. Lavender, have you been to see your cardiologist?"

I answered back. "No, but those little white pills you gave me worked fine, and I need some more."

With my new file in her hand she responded. "Dr. Jones wrote on your record that you have congestive heart failure, and you were to report to a cardiologist right away."

I told her that I did not understand all of what she had told me. No one told me I had congestive heart failure. She rushed me in to see Dr. Jones. He became stern with me about not following his directions.

My reply to Dr. Jones was, "With the changes in primary care and referrals, why don't you professionals decide exactly where I need to be and I will be certain to go there."

He called Dr. James Miller and told him my recent history. There was a pause as Dr. Miller spoke to him. When the conversation was finished, Dr. Jones spoke not a word to me but gave his nurse instructions to put their Med Trends records in an envelope and have me report to Athens Cardiology by 1:00 p.m.

I discontinued my assignments for that day and went straight to the office to let them know of the recent revelation. I was at Dr. Miller's office on time, and they took me straight to him. Instead of the normal appointment rooms, I was taken to his plush office where he met with me.

The first thing he asked was, "Why did you go to Med Trends instead of coming here?"

My response was, "I at least got to see a doctor when I thought I needed one."

His response was, "They can't put you in the hospital."

I said, "I did not know that I needed to go to the hospital."

He said, "That is where you are going. Can you go now?"

I said, "Yes, sir, if that is where I need to be."

At the hospital I was taken in right away and given a room, and IVs were started. This was all new to me. Intravenous diuretics were given along with a measuring urinal. By evening I was feeling much better and inquired about going home.

The nurses chuckled at that absurdity. "You're not going anywhere for about a week." That was news to me also.

The next day Dr. Miller visited me and sat by my bed with his legs crossed with my medical file in his hand. After several questions about my lifestyle, he gave me some very strict instructions.

Then he asked me. "Do you know what congestive cardiomyopathy is?"

I said, "I think that is a heart disease that will get a person a new heart."

Dr. Miller grimly nodded affirmatively. I was devastated. But Dr. Miller made the best of the harsh news with the plans to manage my disease much closer.

After the first heart transplant in 1967, the patient lived for only eighteen days afterward mainly because of rejection factors. By 1987 some patients were living up to fourteen months as more knowledge of rejection was obtained. Cyclosporine contributed greatly to improving the rejection factors.

I was in the hospital for five days and lost twenty-five pounds of fluid. I lost from 250 down to 225 pounds. I was put on the best medications known for my condition and returned to work. The heart doctors were relentless in trying to get my BMI (body mass index) to 185. I had not been 185 since 1968.

After my heart condition had digressed into congestive cardiomyopathy, the time between hospitalizations shortened. In 1989 it had not been ten years since my visit to Dr. Tallmadge's office.

It was July 24, 1991, as I returned from North Georgia Hydro Operating Headquarters. It was 4:50 p.m., and I was ten minutes from the Athens office and quitting time. I was on Newton Bridge Road within one mile of the office. I noticed a Mexican immigrant pushing his bicycle upgrade on the opposite side of the road. He collapsed face down on the paved entrance to his mobile home park. I pulled over and immediately radioed into the division operator where my office was located. I told them to send an ambulance to my location. I then left my vehicle to render aid. I shouted to the fast developing crowd not to touch him and ran to check for his carotid pulse. There was none. I rolled him over as a nurse dressed in a white uniform from somewhere appeared and knelt beside me.

She said, "We have got to do something! Do you know CPR?"

I replied. "Yes."

I agreed to do the compressions if she would breathe for him. As we began to try and resuscitate him, I heard the ambulance siren from the hospital a mile and a half away.

The hot summer sun was beating down relentlessly on the black pavement and my back. I began to sweat. It seemed like forever before the ambulance pulled very near to where we were working. When the EMTs got out of the ambulance, I expected them to take over. Instead they shouted, "Continue CPR!"

I was already beginning to fatigue. The EMTs were making their preparation to take over by removing a gurney from the ambulance and gathering their equipment.

Finally they shouted, "Stop CPR!"

I stood up as the sweat dripped from me. I watched as the EMTs worked with the victim. They applied the paddles and high voltage several times and then with a syringe and long needle gave him a shot to the heart and put him on the gurney and away they went with sirens wailing. I turned to thank the nurse for her assistance, but she was nowhere to be found.

My Invisible Friend reminded me. "Don't forget to show hospitality to strangers, for in doing so, some have entertained angels without knowing it" (Hebrews 13:2).

When I arrived at the office, Bill Christopher was still there waiting on me. He wanted to know the details. I felt the need to wash my hands and face over the utility sink in our storeroom. I became shaky and emotional. Bill did not make it clear why he wanted to know the details of my efforts. The next morning I sadly discovered the victim was pronounced deceased two hours after arriving at the hospital.

Apparently, the Southern Company wanted their employees to become more involved with the public. The executive vice president of the Southern Company and all of Georgia Power's Telecommunications superintendents were invited to a grand luncheon in my honor at the Georgia Powers Administrative Office in Atlanta, Georgia. The executive vice president sat at the head of a long table, and I was seated on the other end. After the luncheon they presented me with a CPR Life Saving Award plaque and asked me if I wanted to say anything.

I became emotional as I said, "But he died. I just wished I had prayed for him, but there was no time."

They tried to make me feel better by reassuring me that I had given him my best.

Two weeks later I was working at our annual pork BBQ at Antioch Christian Church. I was dressed in my dad's old faded overalls in the hot August sun. Once again I was drenched with sweat. I leaned against a nearby pickup truck with my head on my forearm. Stan Lowery had been helping me to lift hot black cast iron wash pots half full of chicken broth.

In a concerned manner he asked. "Billy, are you OK?"

I replied that I would be OK after I caught my breath. I went over to the air-conditioned fellowship hall and took a break.

By Sunday afternoon the wheezing was prevalent. I did not sleep at all that night. The only way I could get relief was to sit up in a chair and lean to one side to breath. I kept looking at the clock as morning approached. By 4:00 a.m. it was evident I could not go to work on so little sleep. I called the cardiology group. Dr. Sinyard was on duty. I could hardly speak for having to catch a breath.

He asked me yes and no questions, and after about three or four yes and no answers he gave me his instruction. "I am at Saint Mary's hospital as I speak, but I will be going to Athens Regional Hospital shortly. I will meet you there. When you arrive they will be expecting you. I'll see you in a bit."

His instructions were accurate and precise. When I approached the registration desk, nurses were standing by with a wheelchair and rushed me into the ER. Right away they started the intravenous diuretic. Dr. Sinyard appeared by my bed and asked me why I waited so long to come in.

I replied. "I thought after my last hospitalization I was already taking the best medication available."

He said, "You are, but with the nature of this disease, the oral medication ceases to be effective."

Within minutes I was shedding the excess fluid and feeling much better, but I was in for another long stay. I lost another twenty-five pounds of fluid and was given an echo cardiogram.

There were two nurses trained to give the echo test in Athens, and I was poking fun with them as we talked about all sorts of things.

When Dr. Outz came to read the results in their presence, their demeanor changed from lightheartedness to one of serious and utter surprise. Both their mouths dropped open when Dr. Outz asked me if I had been keeping up with the heart transplant program.

My answer may have seemed flippant, but it was truthful when I responded, "I only know what I have heard on the Public Broadcasting Network."

He then said, "We are sending you to the Emory Clinic for Heart Failure in Atlanta. It is time for those boys to take a look at you."

I asked. "Why the big change?"

He answered. "On a scale from zero to sixty, your ejection fraction (the ability of my heart to pump blood) is eighteen."

My heart was only 30 percent efficient.

Cheryl and I made the first of what was to be many trips to Emory University Hospital. My first appointment was with Dr. Andrew Smith, the director for the Center for Heart Failure. There was no way I was prepared for what I was about to hear.

After a moderately long wait, Dr. Smith, in a doctor's fashion, rushed into the room where Cheryl and I were waiting. He immediately went to work listening to my heart through his stethoscope.

After a few minutes, he hooked his stethoscope around his neck and said the words I will never forget. They became permanently etched into my consciousness. "Mr. Lavender, three out of four men your age with this disease gets worse and dies."

He had my attention. With our eyes locked on one another I asked him. "What about the other 25 percent?"

He realized at that point he had come on pretty strong and paused as he sought some way to say it easier. He stammered a bit saying, "They, uh, go into a fibrillation."

He paused as I sought more explanation. "And?"

"Die," he said.

I looked at my princess across the room and then back at him. "Dr. Smith, are you trying to tell me I am dying?"

He said, "You are, unless we do something, and that is why you are here."

I don't reckon that it mattered, but I sure did not feel like I was dying. Cheryl took it like the champion she is. I later found out she was really broken inside but did not dare to let me see it. She is an incredibly strong and faithful wife.

I was about to begin a school like none other I had ever attended. Between 1992 and 1993 the clinic would put me through a series of test every quarter in their effort to find some way to save my life. They first made me understand that the usual degenerative process would transpire in shorter and shorter increments. I was at the two-year mark. At eighteen months I would need what was called a tune-up with intravenous diuretics and medication adjustments. Then again at twelve months, again at six months, again at three months, and then they said, "We will keep you until we can find a matching heart or until the inevitable occurs."

My next visit to the clinic was an all-day event to meet with seven different professional groups and their associated phases of the heart transplant program. I met with (1) social workers, (2) all the nurses on the transplant team, (3) a psychiatrist, (4) clergy, (5) insurance personnel, (6) social security, (7) the actual surgeon. The two most interesting of the seven were the psychiatrist and the surgeon.

The psychiatrist wanted to know my thoughts on suicide and how I felt about receiving a woman or a black man's heart. I understood the reasons for the questions and had no problem with any of it. The surgeon made a comment that caused me to give it a great deal of thought afterward.

He listened to me as Dr. Smith had done and said, "Yep, I'll see you again about midnight some night."

I asked him why he had said "midnight."

He said, "It always happens at midnight."

When I considered the coordination and preparation it took to bring everything together, possibly from several thousand miles away, settling on the hour of midnight made a lot of sense.

# The Heart Transplant Candidate

My next appointment was in January of 1993. This was the first of four quarterly visits. Before we went any further, I had to be tested to see if I was a candidate to receive a heart. So many factors for a successful transplant were involved; my body had to be perfectly receptive. They would not waist a donated heart on anything less. At that time in medical technology, the transplanted patient's life expectancy was ten years. I looked at that time as surely better than the alternative. I became very anxious about receiving the results of the strenuous tests I had gone through for candidacy.

The blizzard of 1993 blew in on March 12. Since I had a full size 4x4 Bronco, I was dispatched to Madison, Georgia, to find a break in a five hundred-kilovolt transmission line feeding the city. At the Madison operating headquarters, I was given a line crew and our assignment. The wind and snow were terrible. The line crew and I stood in a circle around the operating manager. After we had received our instruction, we all looked at one another in silence. The crew was looking back at me.

I said, "Well, fellows, we are going to ride as far as we can."

At this point with my heart disease I was a pretty sick individual.

We entered the transmission right of way at the top of a hill. We slowly went downgrade to the first obstacle. The snow was at least a foot deep at the bottom of the hill. I could not be sure at the lowest point what lay before me and out of sight. Was it just a dip, a creek, or gulley? It was all covered in snow. I got out of my vehicle and walked to the bottom and jumped up and down with the full weight of my body in hopes of getting a feel for what lay beneath. It appeared to be firm enough that I could make it across with a little momentum. I gave the Bronco the gas, but it bottomed out right away.

I was embarrassed, but there was nothing to do but call in for help. We were told to climb back to the top of the hill where an abandoned house was and take shelter until someone could be sent to pick us up. Everyone was too busy to come right away. The trek back up the hill was very difficult for a healthy man, much less a heart transplant candidate. After an hour or so, we were picked up and taken back to the headquarters. My vehicle was left there for the two subsequent weeks before it could be retrieved.

When we arrived back at the operating headquarters, Randy Kittle was there to take me home. I wasn't feeling very well and felt somewhat useless. When we arrived on Oliver Bridge, the road was barely passable. When we got to our hill, my driveway was impassable. We devised a plan for me to get inside the house. With my flashlight in hand I struggled to climb our hill. Randy waited at the bottom of our hill and watched my flashlight. I was really afraid of collapsing in the snow, and if no one was watching it would be a fatal mistake. If for any reason I could not get into the house and Randy left, the end result would be the same. His signal was to watch for me waving my flashlight after I had contacted Cheryl in the darkness. When Cheryl unlocked the door, I waved the flashlight for Randy to go.

However, there was a bright side to this sad story. When the performance evaluations were in and the raise percentages were given, I was called back into John's office. He handed me a $5,000 bonus check. I asked what it was for. He said during the blizzard of 1993, the only region within the Southern Company that had every backup generator to remotely crank, report, and operate correctly was ours. Their maintenance had been one of my responsibilities.

He said, "You made me look good."

The check increased my average income for my last five years of employment by one thousand a year. In effect, I am still drawing off that bonus check.

I called the Emory Clinic regularly to see if the results were in and if I had made the transplant list. In May I was given the information that I was indeed a heart transplant candidate. I remember announcing it at the next Antioch worship service as a praise report.

Suddenly and unexpectedly I became emotional as I thought of the person that was alive and well and would die, willing to give his or her heart so I might live. As quickly as my heart broke for that person, I was made aware that I had broken the heart of God.

He whispered to me. "My child someone has already died that you might live and live more abundantly. The thief comes only to steal and kill and destroy. I have come that they may have life and have it in all its fullness. The good shepherd lays down His life for the sheep" (John 10–11). Within this human conundrum, God would perform another miracle in my broken body. Just like with Abraham and Isaac and the sacrificial ram. No one was to receive any of the glory God's only son was to receive.

I was required to wear my pager at all times. Since the company had already assigned me a pager, all I had to do was to give the clinic my number. Pagers in that day randomly went off. Prior to making the list, it went off all during working hours. I could easily screen the incoming numbers and voices. Now every wrong number and interference from drug dealers, etc. caused me to be on edge all hours of the day.

The next quarterly test was a right/left heart cauterization to check the pressures inside my heart. They entered through the groin to ultimately find their way to my heart. Dr. Ludwigson, Dr. Smith's assistant, commented that my coronary arteries looked great. After that procedure, I had to lie motionless for several hours while the blood clotted around the incision.

During that time Dr. Smith once again confirmed my ejection fraction as being eighteen. Before and after talking to me, I noticed the nurses walking by my cubical peeking in at me giving me the concerned look.

Soon after Dr. Smith left my cubicle, one of the nurses entered and asked me. "How long have you been out of work?"

Georgia Power was going through workforce reduction, and it made me chuckle. I told her, "I haven't been out of work. I have been bursting my tail trying to hang on to my job."

She said, "You had better slow down! Most patients with an ejection fraction as low as yours are not working at all."

That was the first time I had given any thought to my company benefits. So as to have another "arrow in my quiver," I asked, "Do I qualify for total disability?"

She asked me. "Didn't Dr. Smith talk to you about that?"

I said, "No."

She asked me if I would like for him to talk to me about it and I replied, "Yes."

She located Dr. Smith and had him to return to my cubicle. When he arrived he asked me, "Do you have questions about disability?"

I asked him if I qualified for total disability and his response was, "Yes."

The details in his explanation were that my total disability was contingent upon my ejection fraction. Social Security did not consider an ejection fraction above twenty-two as being low enough for total disability thus eliminating it from consideration. With my ejection fraction being so close to that parameter, any improvement to my health would put me back into the workforce whether I was ready or not.

At that moment I realized my Lord and I had become the only real advocates for the decision I would make about my family's future.

Dr. Smith told me if at any time I felt I could not continue to meet the requirements of my job to fax him a letter and he would fax back to me a disability commencement date. That would be the very first step in the process. That date would be what the human resources department at my company would need to move forward with my claim.

Bill Christopher retired in 1992, and my good friend and former supervisor, John L. Schofill IV, took the superintendent's position. He thought it was best if I was taken off the road, so he put me behind a desk. I was becoming a liability to the company. That became a big factor in the decision-making process. So much of what I enjoyed about my job was the freedom afforded in working independently and providing a necessary service to the company in the field throughout the region. Another factor was "workforce reduction." Where would I be if the company no longer needed my services, and I was put on the street with no income? Though the law had been amended to protect against that, the company had some obligation to assist me through my hardship, but I could not totally depend on that either.

After eighteen years with the company, I had become 100 percent vested. I was entitled to the total benefits that any of the other retired employees were receiving if my condition merited the entitlements. John had complimented me a few months prior with a statement that I was the best microwave technician he had. He assured me he had my back when it came to employee reduction. However, I would still have to make another major decision about my future.

Soon after the blizzard of 1993, the weather turned fair, and it became a beautiful spring. By then a line crew had retrieved my Bronco from the gulley on the transmission right of way. I asked for a vacation day to go fishing. As I entered the bypass from the onramp, a small white pickup truck crashed into the rear end of a car that had stopped abruptly in front of it. It was a horrible collision. I continued to pull forward slowly until I reached the overpass in front of me. The traffic backed up rapidly from where I was parked.

As I had done the previous summer when the Mexican immigrant had collapsed, I called in for an ambulance and explained I was rendering aid. The collision was only four blocks from the hospital. As I ran to the small white pickup truck, a woman had left her car from the other side of the bypass. We both arrived at the truck at the same time. I tried to open the driver's side door, but it was jammed shut. The driver's chin was on his chest, and he was having difficulty breathing. But he was at least breathing. I noticed below his knees and halfway down his shins, both legs were compound fractured with the bone exposed through his trousers. His feet and ankles were bent back toward the front seat.

I told the woman beside me to let me know if he stopped breathing as I started for the occupants of the other vehicle, about fifty yards away.

About halfway to them she shouted to me. "He stopped breathing!"

I ran back to her and attempted to open his airway by lifting his head while pushing strenuously against his forehead. He started to breath. I held that position, as once again, I could hear the ambulance sirens nearing our location. A policeman and another witness were standing close behind us talking about baseball spring training. It was annoying.

When the EMT came to our aid, he said, "Let me show you an easier way." He adjusted my grip on his head and tried opening the door.

I told him the door was jammed, so he rushed to the other side saying, "You'll have to help me get him out."

I said I would.

The EMT knelt on the seat and gripped him under the arms with his hands and began to pull him toward the passenger door. I leaned through the driver's side window and gripped him behind his knees and lifted and shoved his torso as his broken ankles and feet dangled loosely. On the other side of the vehicle, another EMT assisted in putting him on a gurney.

Just as quickly as I had become involved, it was all over. There was nothing else for me to do. It was time to go fishing. Of course, I did not feel much like fishing after that. The bypass on my side was free of traffic. Behind me the traffic was bumper to bumper and at a standstill. I walked to my Bronco and slowly left the scene as the EMTs continued to work with the victim on the asphalt.

The next morning, I called the highway patrol to see if the victim had survived, and they would not give out any information, so one of my peers suggested that I call the newspaper. I called the Athens Banner Herald. They took my number and called me back in about five minutes. The victim's name was Joe Brown. They told me what hospital he was in and his room number. I called Joe Brown. He answered the phone.

I asked him. "Do you know who I am?"

He guessed. "The public defender?"

I chuckled and said, "No, I am Billy Boyd Lavender, and I was the first on the scene of your accident yesterday, and I wanted to know how you were getting along."

With that Joe Brown said humbly, "You saved my life."

I rejected such a rush to judgment and said, "I don't know about that."

But he said, "I do. You saved my life."

I asked him why he was so sure of that.

He said, "The EMTs told me they had to resuscitate me two times on the bypass before I was put in their vehicle."

I thought, *isn't that just like my Lord?* Last year they write me up in the papers and throw a big luncheon and give me an award and the victim dies. This year he blesses my heart with a saved life and no one but God and I know it, just like it ought to be. However, I learned a life lesson from these two events. God receives all the glory for his intervention, and my ascribed role was rewarded with abundant life.

# A Fork in the Road

Off the road and in the office afforded me more time to talk to John about my future. Ultimately John canned a phrase to everything I seemed to ask. "Sharpen your pencil," he would say. After a while I did just that because I knew he was getting tired of the topic. I began to contact all the appropriate personnel to collect every iota of information so I could make an informed decision. We had just purchased a 1991 Ford Explorer. With the company stock that would be released, I could pay off the car. As a benefit, the IT group of the Southern Company had the same benefits as all linemen. There was a basic formula that would ensure that any employee that became disabled while on the job could receive 90 percent of their salary until age sixty-five with the formula applied.

    I was unaware of how few professional people there were whose job it was to assist employees with hardships. On the other hand, I was made acutely aware that the benefits were there but I was the only one who could ask the right questions to get the ball rolling. After I had asked all the right questions and got all the right answers, I put my own financial figures into my calculations. I made $42,000 annually in 1993. So long as I remained totally disabled, with the formula applied I would receive $37,500 annually until I turned sixty-five. When I retired at age sixty-five, I would no longer receive disability benefits but receive my retirement pension from the company with Social Security benefits remaining the same. After sharpening my pencil it was doable.

    I was becoming "stir crazy" working behind the desk, and I was driving everyone whose job it was to sit behind a desk crazy. I asked our secretary to call the human resources department and arrange a meeting. The meeting did not last long because I could not give them a date of disability.

After the meeting I asked the secretary to help me prepare a "fax letter" to Dr. Smith. Within a week I received his "fax letter" with a disability date of July 17, 1993. Every factor that influenced any benefit was retroactive to that date. I first had to apply for short-term disability and utilize that benefit before applying for long-term disability.

I gathered the family together and explained that financially nothing would change but Daddy could no longer work.

Within the various parameters of the disability formula was a benefit that I never thought of or thought I would need. Every day of unused sick leave and unused vacation were totaled and paid in full with a sizeable check. I would have to remain totally disabled for two years on short-term disability before I could apply for long-term disability. When I started long-term disability, the Social Security Administration sent me forms every eighteen months for the doctors to sign and return for proof of continued disability.

My transition out of the workforce went smoothly. I never saw a judge or had to jump any of the expected hurdles that come with total disability. The true fact from my diagnoses was I would either get better and return to work or die. I don't think anyone thought I could maintain a quality of life for an extended period. But those folks didn't know and serve the kind of God I serve.

By October of 1993, I was completing my quarterly checks at the Emory Clinic for Heart Failure. Attending at this appointment was three cardiologist and two nurses. The doctors were Dr. Smith, Dr. Ludwigson, and a physiologist cardiologist. I was being prepared for another test. I was wired on both arms and chest. As they were about to put the oxygen mouthpiece in my mouth, I spoke, "May I say something?"

They replied, "Sure."

This was my prophetic statement. "You are going to find out what is wrong with me now."

They responded, "Why do you say that?"

# IT CAN'T BE LUCK

My answer was, "I have had this condition all my life, and this is the first time I have been on a treadmill. It is obvious that you are going to run me out of the back of this machine. If that monitor is worth anything at all and if you are watching it closely when I leave the treadmill, you will see what I have been living with. That is my problem."

They said, "Fine, give us eight minutes."

I told them, "You're not going to get eight minutes."

They said, "Well give us all that you have."

I said, "I will give you my best."

The nurse placed the oxygen in my mouth as the other nurse prepared to flip the signs I was to read. The treadmill began to turn slowly. I would shake my head negative or affirmative to the degree of difficulty I was having. After about two minutes into the test, we were in the difficult range and try as I might I went out the back end. The nurse caught me before I fell. The doctors were beside themselves with jubilation as they pointed to the monitor.

"Right there, right there," they said.

Dr. Smith said to the nurse, "Have him put on his shirt and send him across the hall."

I was still panting rapidly as she helped me put on my shirt. While I was still buttoning my shirt, I walked into the next room.

With a proctor stick, Dr. Smith pointed to the center of a large colored cross section of a heart. He spoke. "Do you see that small purple spot right there? That is called the interventricular septum. There is a procedure available today that is 90 percent effective, and if you agree to have it done to your septum, you may not have to be transplanted."

My immediate response was, "Do you want to do it right now?"

He chuckled. "Take no more Coumadin, and return in three days, and we will do it."

I thought to ask, "What is the percentile of that percentage based upon?"

He said, "Fifty. Only twelve have been done in Georgia and fifty in the world. Only one doctor is skilled to do it thus far."

Ninety percent of fifty was not as good as one hundred, but none of that changed my mind. I was ready to be the fifty-first person in the world to have a "partial node ablation" by laser.

Three days later when I arrived per instructions given by the clinic, I was received by a host of hospital personnel and a wheelchair. One of the personnel gave me a stack of papers about an inch thick for me to read and sign. Obviously I could not read all that technical "mumbo jumbo," so I flipped through them to the place I was to sign. If I wanted these folks to help me, I had to not only trust in the Lord but also give them whatever consent they needed. I used every minute of the time it took from then to when they placed me on the operating table to sign papers.

After a few minutes everyone was in place. They numbed my groin and inserted the laser catheter. I was conscious during the whole procedure. I watched the overhead monitor as the slender catheter wiggled its way through my body and disappeared into the area of the interventricular septum.

Dr. Langberg said, "We're ready to get started. You may feel this."

My response was, "Give it your best shot."

Unbeknownst to us all, that was a prophetic and imperative command. The normal course for the ablation procedure was to return in six months and finish what needed to be done. The interventricular septum, when scarred by the laser, would provide a filter to keep electrical signals from my brain reaching my heart. At that moment God took control of everything.

When Dr. Langberg pulled the trigger, I likened it to a weld machine with current turned to high. The welding rod will stick until it is either broken away or the current is reduced. I jumped as if I had been shocked with paddles. I spoke immediately on the heels of the moment. "I don't know if I was supposed to feel that!" "But I did!" Everyone around the operating table fell backward, and the lights seemed to go dim.

When I awoke the nurse's face was upside down in my face. "Mr. Lavender, it did not go as we had planned. You will not be able to go home today. You will be hospitalized until further notice."

My comment was, "I figured something went wrong." How wrong I was. Everything had gone perfectly. No one knew at the time, but God had performed a miracle. The procedure had gone just as perfectly as he had intended, but my heart rate was thirty-nine bpm.

I had been informed that the downside of the operation was to receive a pacemaker if too much of the nerve center was inadvertently removed. Within the huddle of those brilliant minds attending me that day, God spoke to them. "Mr. Lavender takes a tremendous amount of maintenance drugs. Before we move further along, make him go 'cold turkey' for three days and for the time being, put in a temporary pacemaker to see if his heart rate rises."

I attribute that to an act of God. He had knocked my heart rate down to thirty-nine beats per minute. He already knew when the drugs were out of system my heart rate would raise to normal.

The next morning as uncomfortable as I was, I was a bit cranky but put on my best behavior. I felt like a human pincushion. I was awakened from a miserable sleep to find a host of brilliant doctors around my bed. Dr. Smith knew how to deliberately push my buttons to get a response from me. I answered him, and they all burst into laughter.

Dr. Smith then said, "See what I mean?"

I still do not know exactly what he meant by that, but I think it was good.

The first day after the procedure, the physiologist checked my pulse rate. It had risen to forty-nine. The second day my pulse rate had risen to fifty-nine. The third day when she checked my pulse rate it had risen to sixty-nine. Like one would check oil with a dipstick, with a small piece of gauze she pulled the catheter of the temporary pacemaker from the apex of my heart, put a Band-Aid over my jugular vein and said, "Looks like you can go home." She gave me a new regiment of medication, and I was on my way. For the next twenty years, my heart's ejection fraction would improve to normal, but I would live with continuous A-fib and have to take Coumadin.

My church family was not aware that I had been hospitalized. I was back at church the next Sunday. I was able to offer a praise report to the congregation. I was much much better.

I was put on a six-month checkup at the Emory Clinic until my retirement. I did not mind the drive to Atlanta every six months at all.

Just as the doctors had predicted my ejection fraction started to improve right away. Within a year my heart had strengthened to twenty and soon was outside the parameter for total disability. However, an unknown side effect of the partial node ablation began to manifest itself. Once again I was put on the treadmill test. This time I performed much better as they expected I would; however the ability of my heart to consume oxygen had greatly diminished. After the test the nurse showed me the red-lined graph on the monitor. The oxygen I was consuming was way below the normal level. If I were in an environment of pure oxygen, the level would never rise. Thus, another parameter for total disability had taken the place of the one for the ejection fraction.

When friends and relatives asked me how I am getting along with my health, I best described it as being gratefully strapped in second gear. I can walk. I can talk. I can take care of myself. I cannot run. I cannot get in a hurry. It sure beats the alternative.

# IT CAN'T BE LUCK

# The Seed Stock Hobby

In 1991, at age eighty-two, my dad bought his last bull. His small herd of about thirty cows was developed from line breeding with bulls from his own stock. He was thinking seriously of discontinuing cattle completely, but I encouraged him to purchase one more purebred Hereford bull to help me get started with my own seed stock program. He purchased a fine young bull. He was still too small for service in 1991 but would serve vigorously the years thereafter. He grew to be five feet tall at the shoulder and weighed 2,200 pounds.

Cheryl and I purchased two registered heifer calves from a seed stock grower in Ball Ground, Georgia, the same year. Over the next several years we purchased two more full-grown cows with excellent pedigrees. They were not cheap. We enjoyed attending the seed stock sales around Georgia in the fall of the year. The local growers threw a big invitational party each harvest season. One big grower would not let another big grower outperform their gatherings. Entertainment from popular country stars performed after a feast in the evening before the sale and again before another BBQ and dinner on the grounds the day of the sale.

During this period Cheryl worked at the Animal Sciences Unit for the University of Georgia. I was kept informed on the stock they would be selling and got a close look at one very fine heifer. We purchased her for $1,700 at their next sale. Another fine cow became our donor dam, and we purchased her for $1,500. Our neighbor, Russ Page, was the owner of Reproductive Progress just a mile from our house. He could flush the eggs from our best females and fertilize them with semen from around the state. My first flush yielded seven calves.

To flush successfully I had to make arrangements with a local dairyman to freshen seven of his heifers and pasture them through the winter. The plan was for me to return them to his dairy after nine months ready to milk. The seven dairy heifers became the recipients for my seven fertilized eggs. The offspring would be purebred Hereford stock of my choosing. Our small herd grew rapidly totaling about twenty brood dams, one herd sire, and their offspring. The largest number of cattle we ever had at one time was thirty head.

Another necessary asset for this kind of reproductive progress was to have nurse cows available for the purebred calves. High-lactating dairy cows were often culled because of poor udder shape, but they made excellent nurse cows. I bought one crossbred Holstein lactating at about eight gallons per day and another jersey cross lactating at four gallons per day. Between the two udders there were eight teats, eight quarters, and six gallons of rich warm milk available for seven calves at each feeding twice a day.

It was one of the more pleasurable parts of our hobby. Most of the time "it is not nice to fool Mother Nature." Successfully tending a brood of purebred Hereford baby calves was something to see. There were four calves nursing on one cow and three on another.

Tending the herd was good therapy for me, but the cost of leasing pasture, financing a hay crop, the purchase of a cattle trailer, and a used tractor and bush hog made it a breakeven proposition. Sales from the herd created a small cash flow, and we kept beef in the freezer, which was a fringe benefit. Most of the time our stock was purchased for breeding purposes.

One time a buyer drove from middle Georgia and bought my entire crop of yearling heifers. He saw they were in good shape and told his wife who was sitting in their Lincoln luxury car, "Mama, write him a check."

When I asked him what he was going to do with that many heifers he said, "I am going to butcher them for Christmas presents."

What could I say? I said nothing but thanks.

We raised Polled Hereford Seed Stock for twenty years between 1991 and 2011. The end product of breeding management came after fifteen years of selective breeding. Most of the brood cows were aging and so was I. We artificially inseminated the aging cow we had purchased as a heifer at the university sale to one of the top sires in the industry from J. L. Hadden's ranch in middle Georgia. That pairing produced our finest herd sire. His offspring was very consistent genetically. We called him "Our Mr. Victor."

After four years our Mr. Victor developed a foot problem on one of his back feet, which made him useless as a herd sire. In order to keep our cows settled, we transitioned to a black Angus bull, also purchased at a University of Georgia Animal Sciences Sale. The "Black Baldy" offspring brought top dollar and was just what the beef industry wanted.

Above Red at 8 months
Below Red at 36 months
Right Cheryl with Red's dam

Above Red and Me in Griffin
Left Red/Sharp Vote & The Eskimo kiss

Red at eight months, Red's dam and Cheryl, Red at thirty-six months, Red at five years and the Eskimo kiss

# A Sire for Red

Watkinsville, Georgia, is the Oconee County seat. When Cheryl bought Red as a six-month-old filly in 1985, many of the county roads were still unpaved. Soon after 1985, Oconee County became one of the fastest-growing counties in the state. While we still had some less traveled roads, the horse lovers would create horse-riding events called "Wagon Trains." The organizers would pick a route and start on a Friday afternoon and end on a Saturday night, camping along the way until the final destination was reached. At the last stop, usually late on Saturday afternoon, the event was terminated with a cookout with the local talent performing country acts on stage as entertainment.

When Red was two years old, she had grown to fourteen and one-half hands. We had her professionally broke to the saddle. We also bought another horse from a riding stable so Cheryl and I both could ride together. To give the horses and us the added experience, we attended some of these wagon trains. Owning two horses was a bit too much for our lifestyle at the time, and the second horse was somewhat frail and my weight would cause the horse to tire rapidly. So Red would not be so alone in the pasture, we decided to sell the second horse and breed Red.

In 1990, our daughter, Susan, was fourteen years old and took interest in tending and riding Red. One afternoon while I had Red saddled up, Cheryl and Susan found Red and me across the road at the neighbor's house. Susan asked if she could ride Red back to the house about a quarter ¼ mile away. I thought it would be OK, so I adjusted the stirrups, and I helped her to get seated.

Just like it had been with me on the Hancock Stallion, the same happened with Susan and Red. They were off in a flash before I could give her any last minute instructions. I jumped in the car with Cheryl, and we raced after them, but they were already out of sight. I was so afraid she might meet a car on Oliver Bridge Road unexpectedly, and I did not want to think of the results. When we reached the top of the hill, Susan had already dismounted and was thrilled beyond measure.

She was hopping and hollering. "Man that was fun!"

I knew exactly how she felt, so what could I say? I remembered my cousin, Sandra, and me on the dirt roads in Americus and how the wind whistled in my ears with the rapid and smooth pounding of the horses' hooves.

When Red was five years old, she was fifteen and one-half hands at the withers. She was stocky, and her quarter horse confirmation was excellent. As interested as I had become in breeding genetics, I researched Red's pedigree. Red came with no papers and was sold as a grade quarter horse. I was curious as to why there was just one grade animal for sale from the university. I tracked down the previous owner and put Red's genealogical history together.

One of the professors at the university was Dr. Hughesner. He was a horse lover and bred championship show mules as a hobby. While looking for a grade female horse prospect to cross with his "Mammoth Jack," he found Red's mother at a horse sale. She was in emaciated condition, but he knew he could restore her health and use her for his breeding program. She was a short horse but long and powerful in the rest of her confirmation. When she was crossed with Mammoth Jack, the mule offspring grew into blue ribbon champions almost every time.

The professor also had a solid red sorrel racing stud that was appendix registered. He had a fine pedigree on both sides, but he had not attained enough points at racing to become registered as a "Running Quarter Horse." He was a beautiful stud at sixteen and one-half hands. His name was "Win More Charlie." On his dam's side was a thoroughbred. On the sire side was another running stud. By an accident, Red's mother and Win More Charlie had a fling, and the result was Red.

Though there were many studs available, we wanted to breed up in size. I had become aware that as a general rule my weight tired the horses more rapidly than a person half my size. Therefore I had come to the conclusion that a larger more muscular horse to ride would solve the problem.

We searched through the magazines and found a thoroughbred stud in Griffin, Georgia. He too was a solid red sorrel named Sharp Vote. He also had an excellent pedigree. Some of the greatest thoroughbred racing studs in the world was in his genetics and not too far back. Almost every racing horse enthusiast is familiar with Bold Ruler, Secretariat, and that genetic line.

Sharp Vote's main genetic contribution was to sire "jumping horses." When we arrived at the stables, Sharp Vote was in his exercise pen kicking up his heels. We did not bring Red on the first trip. We made arrangements and set a date to return to Griffin when she was cycling.

When we arrived the second time the pheromones must have been in the air. I had never heard such communication between horses before. The air was full of neighing and whinnying and excitement. The stalls in the barn came alive. Those horses outside the barn also joined in the chorus.

The owner of Sharp Vote thought it was best if we introduced Red to him without taking him from the barn. From outside the barn we led Red to the window of his stall. It was a beautifully romantic site if you love horses. With their ears forward and their necks arched in a "rainbow fashion" they touched noses in "Eskimo style."

Clumsily they bumped into each other's nose and recoiled rapidly as if they had touched a hot stove. Then they moved more slowly toward each other and gently touched muzzles for a more extended investigation. That was enough for a proper first introduction. To make sure she was settled, we left Red for forty-five days before returning to bring her home.

I really wanted the Lord's blessing on this pairing since we had such a disastrous result with Misty Blue. The only response from my Invisible Friend was found in Psalm 147:10 and Psalm 33:17. He takes no pleasure in the strength of a horse or in human might.

A horse is a false hope for victory nor does it deliver anyone by its great strength. Put in that context and our equine history, it should have been pretty clear to me that God was leading us away from our extreme adoration of horses.

Just like with a strong willed child in human parenting, God was dealing with my strong will as it pertained to horses and music. In both cases instead of an opened door, he had shut and barred the entrance like Noah's ark before the flood.

Learning about horses can take a lifetime. There is much to consider especially if one plans to breed and raise them. The gestation period for horses is eleven months. When Red was six years old, she foaled Sharp Vote's beautiful chestnut colt. Another disaster was on the horizon. Because of a menace called fescue fungus, Red was dry and would not lactate.

The colt would buck and bump Red's udder constantly. It was clear to me he was not getting his "first milk," colostrum. We called a new veterinarian living near us. She gave me injections to give her to start her milk flow. She kept encouraging me that she would start, but the clock was already ticking. We named the colt "Buck" because of his incessant bucking around Red as he bumped her udder. Without being instructed, we bought cow's colostrum milk that would provide the natural antibiotics that newborn mammals need. Buck rejected it. He wanted mama's milk.

Forty-eight hours after Buck was born, I came home from work and Buck was down. I shouted for the children and Cheryl to help me load Buck into our pickup. It was all I could do to lift the one hundred-pound colt and place him in the back of the truck. He was weak, but we still had to hold him down as we raced to the University Large Animal Clinic.

The teaching veterinarian evaluated Buck and gave us the grim news. She told me we were too late, and Buck was already too far gone. She admonished us for not contacting a veterinarian sooner. We told her about the vet that had been instructing us. She took down the necessary information and wrote her a letter of reprimand. That was too little too late for our family. We returned home without

Buck. Red seemed to know something was wrong as she whinnied. She stood motionless as I hugged her neck and wept bitterly.

A friend in the Animal Sciences Department at the university had a stud quarter horse named "Old Man Denarii." He was a son of the famous quarter horse "The Old Man." The Old Man was the only quarter horse in the history of the quarter horse association to have won championships in all categories of quarter horse performance. The Old Man was also a direct son of the famous "Three Bars," a thoroughbred sprinting champion.

As we had done in Griffin, we took Red to Cheryl's friend's house in Crawford, Georgia, for a visit with his stud. After she had settled, we brought her home, happily awaited the new arrival.

This time we took every precaution with Red's health but were still anxious about her lactating performance. Because my dad's farm had better facilities for Red's foaling, we made her a comfortable maternity ward in Dad's barn. The foal was a sorrel filly with a star between her eyes, so we named her Star. Red was so proud of her newborn, and Star provided Red the much needed company we had sought for her.

# Another Talent Show

It was becoming clearer. I was living out my life according to the will of God. There still remained a part of me that tried to reason my way into a recording contract. I was not wise enough in my own understanding to accept the many blessings God had given to my family and be satisfied with his will.

In 1995, another announcement from a Christian radio station came over the air. It was very similar to all the other previous advertisements. The winner of a Southern Gospel Music talent search would receive a recording contract. The location of the show was in nearby Crawfordville, Georgia. Again I started to reason that maybe God intended for me to sing exclusively gospel music and stay away from the tainted secular music of the country songs. I felt like it was worth a try. Maybe the door would open.

The contest lasted all day long at a local gymnasium in Crawfordville. There were many great singers from around the area. At the end of the day, the contest concluded with performances from professional singers and some recent winners. The winner would be announced during the concert and perform at that time. All other participants of the contest would receive a critique of their performance two weeks later through the mail.

At the end of the contest and during the show, it soon became obvious that I had not placed. However, when my critique came in the mail it showed that I had scored very high. There were five or six categories, and each of them was divided into tenths. My performance maxed out in all categories except the last one. Within that category there was a division about breathing. I had learned to sing around my disability and catch a breath at unusual times to be able to hold a note, etc. I knew that electronically in the studio that could be dubbed out. But the judges were looking beyond the studio to future stage performances. When I saw the show at the end of the day, I became more aware of why I had not placed.

The performers were practically doing calisthenics as they sang with great enthusiasm. I knew I could not perform at that level.

After so many years of holding out hope of obtaining a recording contract, I began to think in another direction. Maybe the answer from the Lord about that goal was a simple no. What would be so great for my family or me if I lost them or my life in the process of contractual obligations and the stress of touring performances?

A famous country artist wrote a hit song called "Who's Going to Fill Their Shoes?" The song pertained to the many singers that have come and gone providing the fine music we hear and performances we see.

A line in that song spoke directly to me. "There are a whole lot of singers in this old world but only a few are chosen."

As I began to think that I was not one of the chosen, God corrected my train of thought toward a conciliatory fact. I had been chosen, to do and to be exactly what I was. He reminded me of the twenty-five years I had sung at weddings and funerals and the many solos at worship services and gospel benefits. The number of talented singers with recording contracts was small as compared to the tens of thousands that brought glory to him through their servitude in this manner.

From a Sunday school lesson he also conveyed to me. "If the world could give an example of a successful life it would show you a famous star. However, when God shows you an example of a successful life He shows you a servant."

# IT CAN'T BE LUCK

The Southern Gospel Music Talent Show, Crawfordville, Georgia 1991

# The Donnie Sumner Story

Antioch Christian Church has its share of talented singers and choir members. During the course of a year a committee selects other talent from outside our church to come and perform. One such talented gentleman was Donnie Sumner, the son of Pentecostal preacher and the nephew of the famous bass singer, J. D. Sumner.

During Elvis Presley's climb to stardom, Donnie was a backup singer and piano man for the King of Rock and Roll. In 1976 with his finances depleted and his body emaciated from high drug usage, God saved him and made him a new creature. God changed his music and his health and set him in a new direction.

Donnie would come to Antioch every spring and give a short testimony, sing, and play the piano. From 1985 to 2004 David Perkins had been the presiding preacher for the longest period in Antioch's two hundred-year history. In a discussion with him about my desire to obtain a recording contract, he suggested that Donnie might give me some pointers.

My mother had given me an early model cassette player that had belonged to my grandmother, Cleo. I never used it and thought I would set up a packaged audition and mail it to Donnie. I cued the audition tape and put a sticky note on the recorder saying "push when ready." It was all designed to make it as simple and easy for him to listen to as I could make it.

Intentionally I did not put my return address on the package and wrapped the recorder in a quantity of brown paper that had contained correspondence from Blue Cross and Blue Shield in Columbus, Georgia. What happened next provided final closure of my desire to obtain a recording contract.

# IT CAN'T BE LUCK

David gave me Donnie's address, and I mailed him the package. I never heard back from Donnie, but it was not because he had not tried to reach me. As I had planned, Donnie replied through David. I intentionally wanted the evaluation to come from a third party. The story was not quite as clear when David told it to me, as it was when Donnie explained it the next spring on his visit.

The morning Donnie visited, I shook his hand upon entering the church, and we chuckled at my audition endeavor. He asked me if it was OK if he shared that story with my congregation.

I said, "Sure, I need some clarification on what exactly happened anyway."

His story went like this. "I received this package in the mail wrapped in brown paper and set it aside until I had time to check it out. When I took it into my study and unwrapped it, I found a small cassette player with a sticky note on it that read 'Push when ready.' I was skeptical about what would happen when I pushed the play button but was relieved to hear Billy Boyd Lavender's voice. I took some notes and thought that maybe he wanted his cassette player returned to him and looked for a return address. The only address on the paper was Blue Cross and Blue Shield in Columbus, Georgia, so I put the notes I had written inside and mailed it to that address.

"When the package arrived at the Blue Cross Blue Shield Headquarters in Columbus, Georgia, c/o Billy Boyd Lavender, it immediately became a suspicious package. At first they thought Billy Boyd Lavender might have been a disgruntled customer. They called the Georgia Bureau of Investigations. It was x-rayed and found to have electronic components inside. The GBI took some notes before turning it over to the bomb squad for detonation. Billy's fateful little cassette player was now in very small pieces of an electronic puzzle. Still unsure of just what the mess was, the GBI notified the Tennessee Bureau of Investigation.

"I was sleeping in on Saturday morning when the TBI came to my door. I was half asleep and in my bathrobe. I was quite surprised to see the men in black suits with their badges flashing. My first silent thought was, *I haven't done drugs in a long time. What do these guys want?* The first question they asked was, 'Do you know a Billy

Boyd Lavender?' 'I know of him,' I said. To my relief, it soon became apparent that it had all been a misunderstanding."

    The Lord and I were the only participants in that story that knew just how big of a misunderstanding my efforts to obtain a recording contract had been. That was the final door God would have to shut. After nearly forty years, I finally got the message.

Cheryl and I

# Those Black Little Hands

Antioch Christian Church is a service-oriented church. Within its organization is an active missionary program. For several years during the last part of the twentieth century into twenty-first century, a mission team from Antioch would fly to Jamaica to build a house for a needy person. Their houses were no more than a deluxe version of what we would call a shed. Nevertheless, when we presented the key to its recipient, everyone involved was very satisfied with the end results.

Cheryl and I wanted to go on one of these trips, but I was afraid my health condition would cause more of a burden to the team than one of service. I talked it over with David, our pastor, and we decided there were other areas of service that I could perform if I took my guitar.

After prayerful consideration, Cheryl and I decided to go. The entire team stayed in a gated missionary's home. He and his wife had several bungalows in their backyard. The missionary's house was air-conditioned. The older male members of the team and all females stayed in the missionary's house. The younger men and youth leaders stayed in the bungalows. After we first arrived, David made it clear to everyone that I would be staying in the same bedroom with him and the leadership staff. I thought that was very kind of my friend and pastor.

The week in Jamaica had a structured protocol. To efficiently move the team and accomplish our goals, it had to be that way. We held morning and evening devotionals and prayer before breakfast and after supper. After breakfast the team split up into groups and set about doing different tasks. Near the end of the week, time was set aside for some fun and recreation on the beaches and swimming areas. The night before we left, we dined in an exquisite restaurant on the waterfront.

Each day after the team split up into groups, some went to build the house, and others stayed behind and met with the local Jamaican children at their church for Bible school. A great many children came every day. Cheryl and I were a part of the Bible school staff. I hit it off with the children right away, but I soon learned it was my guitar they were most interested in.

They were a very rambunctious group of young people aging from toddlers to fifteen years of age. They had to be divided into several groups in order for us to have some control over them and thus teach them. There were times the only way the teachers could gain control was to promise them I would play the guitar.

The Jamaican culture displays a wide range of innate musical ability. Deep in their DNA seems to be the ability to keep time and rhythm. When I would play for the children, they would crowd in around me so close I could not strum. It became obvious to me they wanted to be a part of my performance. Little black hands were reaching and touching me and my guitar continuously. I soon discovered I could let them take turns strumming the guitar as I sang and made the chords. Collectively we would select a tune such as "Jesus Loves Me" and allow them to be part of the performance. Those waiting their turn would reach under my elbow in anticipation and place their small warm hands on my forearm as I played. Those little black hands exuded so much love and tenderness it was distracting, but I never forgot the experience.

With as much good as the missionary team brought to the island that week, there seemed to be a strange dark cloud that followed us around. Jamaican culture is riddled with black magic, voodoo, etc. Cheryl's brother, Larry, was also on this mission trip. He was particularly aware of a menacing spirit. We stopped on the mountainside to take some pictures. It was a beautiful scene overlooking the bay area miles below. As Larry stepped back to focus and capture the scene, he inadvertently stepped into the traffic, and another missionary hit him with his automobile. Though it did not seem serious at first, his foot had been broken severely. Though he was taken to the hospital for X-ray and a diagnosis, the doctor said his foot would be OK. He continued to hobble on his foot for two weeks after he returned home. When he finally went to his personal physician, he was put in hard casts for eight more weeks.

 Beginning with September 11, 2001, *this curious onslaught of evil did not go unnoticed by our pastor after our mission trip. Though we were back home in America, horrendous automobile accidents involving our church members with multiple fatalities were occurring within a few miles of Antioch.*

# Sitting in the Mercy Seat

On June 22, 2002, our donor dam calved twins, a bull and a heifer. For reasons only known to Mother Nature, the mother rejected the bull calf. I knew if the calf did not receive colostrum within eight to twenty-four hours, he would die. I had learned to stockpile colostrum in the freezer for such an occasion. I brought the bull calf home and started it on the bottle. I was pleased to see that he was taking the substitute. On June 23, on Sunday morning, Cheryl and I fed the calf again and hurried to the house to dress for church.

It was 9:45 a.m. as Cheryl and I left in our 1991 Ford Explorer. We had our usual discussion about seat belts that Cheryl would not use. She settled in behind the steering wheel. I on the other hand had buckled up out of habit since it had been my company's policy for the eighteen years I had worked for them. We turned from Oliver Bridge Road south onto Highway 15 in route to church about three miles away. Cheryl was unusually quiet as I chattered about how pleased I was with the work the mechanics had done on our Ford Explorer.

The Explorer was eleven years old at the time, but we couldn't afford another vehicle.

I had just said, "When we have the brake job done, it will be like new."

In a perturbed manner Cheryl said, "Bill, you only said that ten times last night."

I looked at her and then back at the road. At that moment and out of sight, a car was approaching us traveling northbound at eighty miles per hour in the slight curve before us. We were traveling about sixty miles per hour. Still three hundred feet away, the oncoming

Ford Maverick lost control and overcompensated after his right front wheel left the pavement. Gravel, grass, and dust flew into the air.

I shouted. "You see him, don't you?"

"Get on the shoulder! Slow down!" Cheryl responded as all four of our tires hit the right shoulder. We were teetering on top of a steep embankment.

Then like a film projector showing stop and start frames in slow motion, the gap between vehicles lessened. At twenty feet the faces of the Mexican immigrants were plain to see through the windshields. Then at ten feet the hood ornaments lined up, and the mouths of the occupants in the oncoming car flew open. Their dark eyes were also wide open with fear. Cheryl screamed. I silently thought this is it. The sudden stinging pain I felt was like none I had ever felt before or since. The sudden stop of our momentum literally attempted to separate my body from my soul. As my body stayed strapped in by the seat belt, my head and arms stiffened and pointed unwittingly and helplessly in the direction of the force. My soul seemed to continue on with the momentum for a short distance and then snapped back into my being.

Then in the sound of the crunching, scraping metal and engine blocks colliding together, a miracle of sorts took place. In the prior three seconds, both vehicles may have broken down their combined opposing force from 140 mph to approximately 120 mph. The lower profile Maverick's force was broken down incrementally as its forward momentum came to a sudden stop. Likewise, our higher profile Explorer lurched vertically like a deer attempting to jump a fence only to be thrown aside like a body slam from a sumo wrestler. Our Explorer rolled over down the embankment. The bending screeching, mangled metal and broken glass gave the combined sound like a demon from Hades. The bright sunshine was shining through the opening in the windshield as the car rocked to silence, upright on all four wheels at the bottom of the embankment. Delayed only for a second, the glass from the windshield collapsed into my lap. I could hear the spewing of the radiator. The total g-force seemed to have split in two directions, vertical and horizontal, breaking down the otherwise more devastating impact.

I was so blessed to hear Cheryl shouting. "My God! What happened?"

I thought, *thank God she made it*. I tried to answer, but Cheryl later informed me that I was silent and she could not see or hear anything.

My lungs were empty of air as I tried to speak. "We have had a head-on collision! Let's say the Lord's prayer!"

I looked in her direction, and the steering wheel she still had in her hands was gnarled around the steering column. Blood clots dropped from her sinus. I grabbed her arm and started to rapidly recite the Lord's prayer. When I spoke the part, "and forgive us our trespasses as we forgive those who trespass against us," the healing began. I lost consciousness.

With nothing but silence about her, Cheryl again shouted. "My God! What happened?"

This time I snapped back into consciousness, painfully took a deep breath, and repeated what I had previously said, but this time I added, "We're going to make it!"

Within seconds the southbound traffic rapidly backed up. Unbeknownst to us my brother, Jimmie, an elder at Antioch, was directly behind us. My sister-in-law, Glenda, put Jimmie out at the scene and drove around the wrecked automobiles on the left side of the highway. She proceeded to notify the church. Tony Powell, a deacon at Antioch, was the first to arrive at our car on Cheryl's side. He asked how bad we were hurt and then stepped back away from Cheryl as the blood flowed from Cheryl's face. I had made a futile attempt to locate Cheryl's cell phone just moments before Tony arrived. I said, "Call 911!"

A crowd quickly gathered. The prayers began first with Jimmie with both hands reaching through the broken windows, one hand for me and one hand for Cheryl. Then a black hand reached through as a black man from another church prayed. More elders were showing up at the scene and more prayers went up.

Andra Dickens was a first responder attending our sister church in Watkinsville, at Union Christian. The call for his assistance came in at 9:50 a.m. Our Sunday school assembly commenced at 10:00 a.m.

There was an eerie quietness in the pews at Antioch. The assembly was about to be called to order, but only a scant few were present. Glenda sought out Eleanor Perkins, the pastor's wife, to inform her. My eighty-four-year-old mother had already arrived at church and was sitting quietly in the pew where she normally sat. Eleanor slid in gently beside her to inform her of our wreck.

Mother then said, "I've got to go!"

Tim Carithers, a deacon, drove mother home by an alternate route avoiding the wreck scene. Later, Sara Downs went by Mom's house and drove her to the hospital.

The further services of Sunday worship were turned over to the youth pastor as the leadership left the church grounds and came to the scene of the wreck a half-mile from the church.

Cheryl still had the steering wheel firmly gripped with both hands and her head bowed as the first of several sirens growled to a stop nearby. The passenger door screeched as Andra Dickens ripped the door aside and unhooked my seat belt and started to feel for where I was injured.

When he put his hand to my chest I shouted. "Don't do that!"

He asked. "Why?"

I told him I had a bruised sternum.

He apologized. I requested that Cheryl be extricated first since I did not have a scratch on me. Miraculously my skin was not broken anywhere, but internally it was a different story.

Larry Anderson, Cheryl's brother, arrived at the scene, as the EMTs extricated Cheryl with the jaws of life. He had to be restrained from entering the ambulance when he saw her spewing blood bubbles.

He shouted. "She's choking on her own blood!"

From my vantage point, I could look up the embankment and see the Maverick on our shoulder of the road, its driver half in the car and half on the shoulder as the EMTs desperately tried to save him. I could not see his passenger. I prayed to the Lord that no one would lose his or her life from this accident.

# IT CAN'T BE LUCK

The loud propeller blades of a helicopter cut the air. *Tut, tut, tut,* as it landed in a pasture just off the right of way. Alejandra Ramos, the driver of the Maverick, was put aboard the helicopter and flown to Grady Memorial Hospital in Atlanta, Georgia. He was resuscitated several times before he arrived at the hospital.

The siren from Cheryl's ambulance wailed as it sped away, and the EMTs prepared to extricate me. They put me in another ambulance with the passenger from the Maverick. As the EMTs were attempting to start IVs in his arm, he resisted saying, "No! No! Senor!"

My feet were beginning to swell in my shoes, so I asked the EMTs to slide them off for me.

They replied. "We have more important things to consider than your feet!"

Twenty-five miles from the scene of the accident, we arrived at the hospital at about 10:10 a.m. The Coumadin I had taken for many years now played an important part in my death or survival. At the hospital my blood was much too thin for them to open me up, so they shot me up with morphine and vitamin K in an attempt to thicken my blood. My attempts at breathing were hampered by stabbing pains. Each breath was accompanied with uh, uh, and uh. The sequence of events from this point forward was understandably muddled. It seemed to me I was being retrieved from a MRI when Dr. Hawk asked me if I had experienced any symptom of appendicitis.

I said no.

My sister-in-law, Shirley, Larry's wife, knew at once the dilemma we faced and the critical nature of our accident. If we survived who would care for both of us after the hospital stay? She took it upon herself to contact the Red Cross—who in turn contacted my daughter, Susan, in Hawaii. She was married to a gunny sergeant in the Marine Corps.

The next time I awakened, the clock on the wall in the emergency room read 4:50 p.m. I was feeling very sick. I could feel myself slipping away. I gazed down at my stomach area. It appeared extremely bloated and tight.

I prayed aloud. "Lord, I don't think I have sinned today, but if I have I ask that you wipe the slate clean and into your hands, I commit my spirit and may your will be done according to the Lord Jesus Christ."

I did not know it then, but the doctors had only given me a 20 percent chance of survival.

Then I shouted loud enough to be heard. "Is my preacher out there?"

Yes was the answer.

I said, "I want to see him."

In came David Perkins, our pastor for the past eighteen years. At his elbow was my best friend of thirty-five years, Mike Marable.

As they looked down, I spoke. "They haven't done anything to me yet. When they do operate, there is a good chance I won't wake up on this side of glory. Will you speak to Antioch for me and tell them that the Lord has given me a chance to make everything right and I am ready to go?"

They tried to encourage me, but David assured me that he would speak on my behalf. Mike later told me that I looked ashen. When the door closed as they left the room, I could feel the sickness worsening. I was sliding down a slippery slope.

This time I shouted as loud as I could. "Yawl better hurry up!"

They did. It was like each one there had been shocked with electricity. Within five minutes, they rolled me away for prep.

The nurses and doctors that were preparing me for surgery were still dressed in their nice Sunday clothes, not in the usual hospital garb. They stuffed a tube up my nose and down into my stomach and placed IVs in both arms. Both the team and I gagged.

My elder brother, Roger, had been on the golf course that morning. He had finished his round of golf and entered the clubhouse. That is when he was told about our accident. Just for a second he shot back at them. "Why didn't you come get me?"

Then he rushed out. From that Sunday for the next two weeks my eldest brother sat just outside ICU and appealed to God for our survival. He only went home to change clothes and freshen up, but he always told me when he was leaving even for a moment. He also kept me informed of Cheryl's progress. He brought me the picture the surgeons had to use to reconstruct her beautiful face. I put it on the wall at the foot of my bed until the end of my stay.

I don't know how long I was in surgery the first time, but Dr. Hawk later told me they operated to explore the extensive internal damage. They found a very distressed appendix. He took care of these pressing issues first. He commented that I might have been going to church, but with an appendix as damaged as the one I had, I would have been in the ER before the afternoon, without the wreck. He told me that he removed my appendix at no charge. They stapled me up and called in the urologist to see if they could save my left kidney. One of the two main arteries connected to my left kidney was completely torn away, and the kidney was mutilated. While I was recovering from that surgery, I heard a familiar voice say, "Daddy, I'm here."

I looked up to see my daughter's smiling face. I knew how far she had traveled and remarked, "Man that was fast!"

The second surgery had failed to stop the internal bleeding. The seat belt had left its bittersweet legacy. The blunt force trauma from the sudden stop caused the seat belt to break the ribs on my left side and collapse my left lung. The jagged bones then punctured my left kidney rendering it useless. On the third day, as I continued to struggle for my life, Dr. Hawk entered my room. My delirious sleep was disturbed when he slid back the curtain.

It sounded just like a shower curtain. "That kidney has to come out," he said.

I asked several stupid questions in support of my kidney.

He just shook his head negatively. "It's mutilated," he said.

Others that have experienced a near-death situation can confirm the veracity of what I am about to write. Over the ten days I was in intensive care, I was intently aware of those that cared for me. It was my observation that about half of the nurses and doctors had the Christian gift of compassion. The other half seemed to perform OK, but to them it was just a job. The way I could tell this difference was through the little things like smiles, tenderness, soft punctures, soft touches, soft voices, etc.

When I came to consciousness after the third operation in three days, my brain was obviously pickled from the tremendous amounts of anesthesia and pain medicine I had received. I was combative, and the nurses had to hold me down with pillows to keep me from bursting open the foot long incision from my sternum to my bladder.

With a half-fried brain, I thought they meant to harm me, so I started quoting scripture and calling out to the Lord. The nurses I deemed to have the gift of compassion appeared normal and caring. However those that did not looked like demons whose faces were painted with black and white salve. They were crying black tears and gnashing their teeth at me. They had fangs like Dracula. It has been easy enough for others that have not been affected by such trauma to dismiss this accounting as a figment of a doped and hallucinating mind. However, normalcy returned with the slightest shift of my head to a compassionate nurse standing beside each of these aberrations.

One of the demonic-appearing nurses said, "Why does he keep saying these things?"

Dr. Hawk whose hands had been inside me every day for three days was washing them in a nearby sink. Apparently he had dismissed the notion that I was going to die and fretfully responded to the nurse. "Because it means something to him!"

With only a one in five chance of survival, I am sure the doctors told the nurses in the intensive care unit to keep me quiet and comfortable and heavily sedated. During my conscious moments in ICU, I was looking for a particular nurse that wore a strange necklace around his neck. Much like a necklace made of bear claws worn by mountain men, this nurse had multiple vials of morphine around his.

He continually made his rounds through the unit. If he saw me looking in his direction he came to my bedside and asked. "Do you need something for pain?"

I would nod yes, and he would lean over near my IV and inject me. Within about thirty seconds I would be knocked out until the next brief and painful moment of consciousness.

After a week in ICU I was awakened one night about midnight as one of the ICU nurses was cleaning around my bladder catheter.

It was the first time I had seen my torso since the wreck. It was solid dark purple from my shoulders to my knees.

During my rehabilitation I learned that the Christian doctors that were caring for Cheryl were also praying for me. They knew that I was at an extremely high risk of having a stroke from blood clots.

Without her seat belt buckled, the extent of Cheryl's injuries was primarily to her face and feet. The miracle of how the vehicles meshed together actually saved her life and pinned her inside the vehicle when it turned over. Most head-on collisions especially occurring on the side of the driver at high speeds, if squarely impacted, are devastating and fatal. The impact will drive the steering column directly into the face and backward severely damaging the cervical and brain area. In this case the upward thrust securely planted her in the driver's seat like an astronaut during a launch. The steering wheel raked upward breaking every bone in her face and knocked several of her teeth out. Her jaw was wired shut, and she received four metal plates to her face during reconstructive surgery. Two of the teeth in the front were knocked out and left a space or hole just right for pureed food that she could draw through a straw.

# Forgiveness and Healing

Cheryl's feet were crushed. It was apparent from the start that the orthopedic surgeons and the maxillofacial surgeons could not or would not work on both ends of her body during the same period. So it was decided that her face would come first, and then as her facial rehabilitation progressed, her feet could then be tended.

Her broken feet were temporarily set and pinned with six spikes in each foot. They looked like nails protruding her soft casts to hold her feet together while her face was reconstructed. Around these spikes on both feet, they wrapped ace bandages that were called soft casts. She sat in a wheelchair wherever she went. My other elder brother, Jimmie, loaned us his Pontiac Safari Station Wagon as a primary transportation vehicle.

Susan was our chauffeur during our rehabilitation. She loaded and unloaded the wheelchair in the rear of the Safari without complaint and drove us both to and from the many necessary follow-up appointments scheduled. On one of the scheduled appointments, the chair was already loaded. Cheryl lay in a fetal position beside the chair in the rear of the Safari. She was using her hand to support her position by placing it on the back of the rear passenger seat. Our three-year-old grandson, little Ben, was on his knees in the rear seat facing his grandmother, and looking at Cheryl directly in the eyes, he patted her hand and said, "I think I'll keep you."

For Cheryl's convalescence, Susan fixed one of our three bedrooms where the sun shone through the double windows. Cheryl was allowed to go home six days after the wreck. Before the wreck she and a few of the women at Antioch were attending sessions at St. James Methodist Church on healing prayer. She sat near the windows and prayed during these long hours for both of us. She became somewhat disillusioned when her healing was not progressing along as she had expected. Though I have not questioned her on the details of these conversations with God, she later revealed this in her testimony.

God revealed to her that forgiveness was a crucial component of complete healing. Not only being forgiven but forgiving others was key to complete physical and spiritual healing. She searched her soul to find whomever or whatever it was she might not have forgiven. Finally she asked the Lord more specifically to reveal to her that person or persons.

One week after my left kidney was removed, Dr. Miller came to give me a report on my heart condition. He said, "Your heart is doing great! Did you sleep well last night?"

I thought for a second or two and said, "Yes I did. I think I rested undisturbed for four hours."

He said, "I can tell. Your color is back. You have turned the corner."

July 5 was my fifty-second birthday, and as a present I was removed from ICU and given a regular room.

Cheryl was not able to come, but my family and friends brought balloons and an ice chest full of soft drinks. I felt ravished after ten days of having a tube in my stomach. I had told them how starved I felt and how thirsty I was. When I actually put this appetite to the test, I could not hold very much. It would take several months to get back to where I was before June 23, 2002.

Unlike the ICU nurses, my caretakers in the regular hospital room were more ridged. They would make me push the limits of what I was able to do for myself. They would put my drinks just out of reach. It seemed it took them longer to respond to the call button. I missed the morphine at regular intervals. I had just started passing soft food and was required to go to the toilet unattended. In order to accomplish this, I carried with me the IV tower, the oxygen bottle, and the tubes and the drainage container for my left lung. The first time I tried this I made it OK until it came time to clean myself. I regretted to have to do it, but I pushed the call button. No one came. After a few minutes I pushed it again. While I was waiting I became faint. I pushed it again and told them, "I'm passing out!"

The next thing I heard was *stat*! *stat*! I could hear the patter of feet coming from all directions.

It was a humbling experience, but I gathered the courage to thank her and told her I was sorry she had to do it. She graciously responded for me not to feel bad, that she did that all the time as part of her job.

By the evening on my fifty-second birthday, I was becoming very restless. The morphine I had been taking had masked the pain that I had been feeling in ICU. It was now prevalent again. All I was being prescribed was an oral pill every four hours. It wasn't enough.

The head nurse for that section was very special. She was compassionate and kind and told me before her shift ended if I needed anything to let her know. I was not restless enough at that time to say anything about the pain. When she returned to work she noticed me squirming in my bed and asked me if I was in pain.

I told her my circumstance, and she said to me, "I can get you some morphine."

Within five minutes she injected me. That was the last morphine I received during my hospital stay. Praise the Lord.

I have had the same barber for fifty years. I asked my brothers if they would contact Herschel Reeves to see if he could come to the hospital to cut my hair and trim my beard. I needed a haircut and beard trim before the wreck. I needed it more than ever at this time. I did not know if he ever did that, but he was glad to do it free of charge.

At my new location, the nurses came in and started moving things around. Usually it was after I had placed my drink, food, and reading material where I wanted them.

I told them. "That is where I had put them."

They told me directly it was their job to get me out of the hospital and back home. That is when I realized why they were making things difficult for me.

The follow-up appointments for Cheryl's crushed feet had begun. She was made aware of the numerous surgeries and rehabilitation she would have to undergo. The process could take up to two and one-half years. Undaunted by the negativity of the remarks, she faithfully believed that God would heal her. Dr. Mcelhannan was the orthopedic surgeon assigned to her care.

During the long hours she spent in the wheelchair, Cheryl sought out the person to whom God was referring and asked God to forgive her for that forbearance. Then one late summer day six weeks after the wreck, another miracle happened.

Susan drove Cheryl to Walmart. As they wheeled around the wide shopping lanes, they happened upon a lady in a flowered hat. Overcome with compassion, the lady approached them.

Almost whispering she asked, "What happened to you?"

Cheryl told her and immediately they realized they both had been studying healing prayer.

The lady then asked, "May I pray with you?"

Cheryl's reply was, "Yes, by all means!"

What happened then I likened to a bubble that descended and engulfed the three of them as they prayed. The energy surged through Cheryl's feet below where the woman's hands were placed. After they prayed, the three became giddy with excitement, each trying to explain to the other what had just happened. Cheryl and Susan could hardly wait for the next appointment with Dr. McClanahan just a few days away.

The day of the appointment and before Dr. McClanahan could speak, Cheryl asked him if he would x-ray her feet.

The doctor balked a little and explained to her gently that she was in for a long process. "You will have to be patient with us through the several operations that we have scheduled. It will not be necessary to x-ray your feet every time you come in for an appointment."

Then much to Susan's credit, our daughter spoke up. "But, Dr. Mcelhannan, you don't understand. Mama's been healed!"

The doctor hesitated then said, "OK," and sent Cheryl to be x-rayed.

I can only imagine the suspense that Susan and Cheryl were experiencing while they waited. Finally the doctor came in with the images. He sat on his stool with two sets of X-ray images in his hand. One was the original image before the miracle at Walmart and the other one that was taken in his office.

He began shaking his head. "I just cannot justify putting hard cast on feet that look that good. Go home and walk pushing the wheelchair in front of you. When you get tired, sit in it."

The importance of forgiving others is paramount when it comes to personal healing. All obstacles must be removed. All sins must be confessed and forgiven. God can then work his miracles.

The numerous naillike spikes were removed, and she was instructed to start walking. She returned to work as Budget Manager at the University of Georgia during the middle of September.

We were so blessed to have survived that horrendous crash with no lasting ill effects. From July 15 to September, Cheryl and I sat on our sofa side by side holding each other's hands. The women in our church signed a list to bring prepared food twice a week. With those deliveries and the normal visitations, at any given time there were several visitors sitting in front of the sofa, laughing, telling stories, and all of us having wonderful fellowship.

Home Health Care was assigned to me since I was required routine blood test even before the wreck occurred. About two weeks into Home Health Care, I asked to be released. The nurse put me through a physical test, and I was left to tend to myself.

On August 25, I successfully pushed my luck and drove my truck to Winterville to get another haircut and beard trim. Hershel nearly fell over when he saw me half bent over and walking through the door of his barbershop. I didn't think much of it at the time, but in retrospect I can recall how slow normalcy returned. First of all the discharge from the hospital was a really big deal. My first drive to the barbershop was encouraging.

Later, however, I made the mistake of tending our herd of Herefords too soon. I got out to stand by my truck as the cattle ran to greet me. They had not seen or heard the truck for two months. The cattle gathered in a boisterous circle around the truck in anticipation of being fed. I became frightened at the precarious and dangerous situation I had caused. I was barely able to crawl back into the cab, and I was emotionally upset at how weak I had become. I stopped by Jimmie's house and told him I was going to sell the cattle because I was unable to tend to them.

He counseled me by saying, "Bill, I would not rush into that right now. You have been through the valley. It will take you some time yet. You have ways to go before you get all of your strength back."

Afterward I limited myself to the sofa and short, easy errands. During the first week in September, on a Sunday afternoon, my best friend, Mike Marable, came to visit and said, "Billy put on your shoes. Get up! You need to get out and see something besides these four walls."

I did, and he was right. He drove me around the countryside to places we both had not seen since we were teenagers.

The church family was wonderful to us during our rehabilitation. Someone was doing something all the time. Whether it was sending cards or bringing food by, it was obvious Cheryl and I were in their prayers and thoughts. Feeling well enough and strong enough to return to our Sunday routine was our immediate goal. When we were seen at Sunday school and worship services on a regular basis, they would know we were over the accident completely.

By September, we started back to church on a regular basis. I was sitting where I normally sit at the rear of the church. Two nice chairs are located in each rear corner of the sanctuary. Cheryl was not in attendance this particular Sunday, so I sat alone in one of the chairs with my head bowed in a prayer of thanksgiving. It had apparently been several minutes before I raised my head. Lined up by my chair were at least a half dozen youth from our church waiting to give me a hug and welcome me back. I could not help but sob with gratitude.

Our pastor, David Perkins, asked if Cheryl and I would share our testimony with the church family. It was early October when we were given a Sunday to share our experiences over the previous three and one-half months. Our survival and healing were obviously supernatural and divine. The end result of such a horrific accident could have left one or both of us dead or maimed for life. We are now so normal in appearance that we must give this testimony for anyone to even know what we have been through. We praise God and are grateful to do it.

We are pressed on all sides, but not crushed; perplexed, but not in despair; persecuted but not forsaken; stuck down, but not destroyed. We always carry around in our body the death of Jesus, so that the life of Jesus may also be revealed in our body. (2 Corinthians 4:8–10)

# Theodore Encounters the Nine Iron

There are many men whose wives are extraordinarily special to them as mates. I have one like that. We have been married forty-seven years and have been through many of life's circumstances. I must say, I would not want to travel those roads again without her, but I might consider traveling them again with her.

If one word could encapsulate her greatest attribute, it would be love. I am a very blessed man to be a part of her love. Pound for pound she's the toughest five foot one inch beauty that ever raised a son and a daughter while attending school and becoming a business manager for the University of Georgia.

We have lived thirty-nine of these years at the same address, a nice home on a hill in eight acres of woods in the country. This has created an environment for every kind of wildlife in the area. Deer, wild hogs, coyotes, raccoons, opossum, rabbits, and squirrels of which at least three of these Cheryl has raised from tiny babies in an effort to save their lives. With each attempt I realized it was a headache for me at the time but a heartache for her later on down the road.

I realized how important pets were to Cheryl early on in our marriage, so much so our home is strategically placed a safe distance from the road for their safety. Her love for animals is not limited to our three horses, two dogs, two cats, and two parakeets. Sometimes the birds and smaller game around our home experience their own personal natural holocaust. Some fall from their nest, and others lose a parent from road kill or hunting.

For example, someone brings to her workplace a litter of baby cottontail rabbits at the absolute cutest state in their growth after the mother has died. Not knowing what to do with them, they were pawned off to Cheryl. For the next several weeks, Cheryl burns the midnight oil, holding each one with her left hand and meticulously feeding each one with an eye dropper full of a concoction she ginned up in the kitchen. I watched her sob each time one would die. In her heart of hearts each one had a name, and just like a mother she could tell them apart. She said they had feelings just like we have.

Another time, the dogs are barking continually all night long. Sometimes this means a snake, possibly a rattler. Not wanting the dogs to get bit, I went out in my pajamas with the flashlight and pistol. Up near the house but under the deck the dogs are growling, salivating, and barking. I shine the light through the cracks in the deck to see enough of what appears to be an opossum. With one shot from my .22, the noise is quieted for the night.

The next day in a rush for the office I walked by the marsupial the dogs had pulled into the backyard. It was moving! But with a closer look I thought it was in some form of fast decay as the belly presented a waving motion. Wrong again. Leave it to Cheryl to discover that the pouch was full of baby possums that needed rescuing.

She had a much more successful outcome with these ancient creatures. Three survived and became quite a handful after they were half grown.

With the help of my daughter, they went online to discover there were "possum lovers" all over the United States. One was given away, one drowned in a drum of rotting calf starter, and another was released, finally, in Memorial Park.

By now I am sure you get a peek into this portion of our lives. Yes, we do have a pet door, and I am quite sure except for the size restriction of our horse, every pet we have is welcome inside. Don't get the wrong idea either, I have grown accustomed to these joint inhabitants, and I think in my own mind they are quite behaved, clean, and healthy.

One evening in the summer of 2011 while reclining in the family room, Theodore came into our lives, breaking the comfortable peace with a high shrill call like that of a bird.

From where I was reclined, I simply shouted. "I think we have another bird in the house."

Cheryl went into full alert until she found him. It was a pink, hairless creature about the size of a mouse. In a word it was ugly. Cheryl broke out the eyedropper.

It was a priority in Cheryl's everyday life for the next eleven months. Miraculously the pink chub responded vigorously, first with hair and then hair on his tail. At the size of a guinea pig he was quite cute. Cheryl would hold him close to her breast and try to get me to hold him. I didn't want anything to do with him.

She gave him the name of Theodore after one of the chipmunks, I suppose. He was looking more like a squirrel every day. After about seven months when his tail had all its hair, he looked like the typical squirrel. Cheryl would bathe him and fixed him squirrel salad every day consisting of fresh fruit, nuts, and vegetables. I would catch heck from Cheryl if I ate the last of the grapes that she had planned to lavish upon Theodore. With such tender love and care, Theodore soon became obese so Cheryl bought him a larger cage and commissioned me to cut just the right stick of firewood to fit inside for him to perch on while he ate.

The little critter did not like me at all. I began to realize he did not like any creature of the male species. Something naturally disconnected in him or rather something failed to connect. He didn't make squirrel sounds like the ones outside. Every time I would walk by his cage, he would grind his teeth and go into overdrive and chew his wire cage. If I placed my hand next to the cage he would manage to jab his needle like claws through and scratch my fingers.

In a sweet voice, Cheryl would say, "Talk to him."

I would think silently. *Yeah, I'll talk to him.*

Soon she bought a clear sphere about the size of a beach ball so he could exercise around the house. Now that was a sight, a squirrel in a clear sphere following Cheryl all over the house.

"Come on, Theodore." And there he went right behind her. Once he bumped into my foot and I felt something tugging at the hem of my pajamas only to find half my cuff pulled into the clear sphere, shredded to pieces.

It was always our intent to eventually set him free if he would go. Maybe he would be one of a kind, letting Cheryl get her hands on him over the coming seasons. We put the cage outside and let him roam around a bit, always making sure to have on long pants and sleeves. He would use us like tree trunks the first time or two, but he soon learned the difference between Cheryl and me.

The time came for us to leave him out all night. He had been hanging around with a bunch of teenage squirrels that evening and did not want to come to his cage. Just like a worried mom with her child on the first date, Cheryl fretted. I told her not to worry that I would give her a squirrel report the next day when I saw him.

The next morning after Cheryl and our granddaughter, Jessie, were gone, I got up to find a teenage squirrel party on our patio. When I opened the sliding glass door the dogs went berserk, and the squirrels scampered in all directions. Theodore wasn't hard to pick out because he was the fat one. In a second all the natural squirrels were in hiding but not the spoiled Mr. Theodore. This was his turf, and he was POd. When I cleared the sliding glass door he came at me with full force. Scratching and biting me anyway he could. I realized in a flash he was not playing around and started to defend myself by throwing him off me and kicking him until I could get back inside. Hmmmm! This could be a problem! Cheryl and I talked it over and decided to give him another chance.

The next morning, I saw him hopping down the driveway, so I followed to see where he was nesting. I lost sight of him when he rounded the curve in the driveway and ran up a tree. Cautiously and in a sweet high-pitched voice, I called to him. "Theodoore, Theodooooore." I was surprised to see him come down the tree and come straight toward me. I was wearing a shirt, a pair of dungaree shorts, and sandals. When he got to my sandals he started chewing on them, then ran up my leg to my shoulder, and down my extended arm to the back of my hand. I was trying to be cool until he tried taking a chunk out of my hand. In a flash he scampered down my back to the pavement. I started bleeding from five spots on the back of my hand consisting of four claw marks and a bite. I slowly started for the house looking over my shoulder becoming more intimidated with each step.

# IT CAN'T BE LUCK

From the corner of my eye, I could see him coming for me with two of his Olympic hops. When he hit the calf of my leg, which would have been a clipping penalty in football, it felt as if he was moving sixty miles per hour. With all the intent he could muster, he buried his claws into my skin and like a four-legged woodpecker, he drove his teeth as deep as he could into the calf of my leg. He dropped to the pavement and hopped to the nearest tree. By the time I reached the house I was bleeding significantly. The blood thinner medications that I was taking didn't help, matters any. Cheryl thanked me for my understanding, but I could see the emotion welling up inside her. She didn't know whether to laugh or cry. How this was affecting my darling bothered me the most.

When I stopped bleeding, I went to my room and retrieved a nine iron from an old set of golf clubs in hopes of defending myself if he came at me again. I put the nine-iron golf club in my truck so it would be handy.

The next day, I was leaving to run an errand when I stepped on to the deck through the backdoor. Out of habit I locked and slammed it shut all in one motion. That effectively locked me out of the house as Theodore came racing down the narrow catwalk on top of the deck rail. I did not have time to unlock the door before he planted all four of his claws into my chest. He was biting and scratching me with everything he had all around my head and neck area. I was able to finally dislodge him and kicked him away like I was punting a football and ran for my truck. I jumped inside the cab and planned my next strategy. Theodore had been hot on my heels and ran out of sight under the truck.

As I thought about this dilemma, I thought about our infant grandson, C. J., and what a mess it would have been if I had him in my arms when I was attacked. I took a chance and hopped out to retrieve my nine iron and relocate it in the cab for an easier access. Before I could get back in the cab, Theodore came at me once again. I haven't played golf in a long time, but I could not have made a more perfect swing. I guess necessity is truly the mother of invention. Just like a blast from a sand trap, I followed through on the swing. The fat tree rodent sailed about six feet and landed on its back with all four feet in the air and lay there still as a church mouse. I still did not trust him. I thought he must be playing possum and planning a surprise attack.

Having hunted squirrels all my life, I have seen them fall from the tops of trees and bounce like a ball and run off. They are also one of the toughest wildlife to skin. I was truly surprised to see him lay there motionless.

I nudged him and questioned. "Theodore?"

I picked him up and shook him. Theodore was graveyard dead.

It was a difficult thing to do, but I confessed to Cheryl what had happened. We had planned to take him to the park soon.

With her emotional and broken voice she asked me. "Did you have to kill him?"

I believe she understood that I really did not intend for that to happen.

# The Shadow of Death

For more than twenty years, I lived with the success of the partial node ablation. I continued to take the same maintenance medications. The doctors were always pleased with my routine checkups. Occasionally over that period of time, I would have an echocardiogram to keep a safe check on my heart disease. My ejection fraction continued to increase until it was back to within the normal range. It had improved about two points per year on a scale of zero to sixty. When the ablation was performed, my ejection fraction was eighteen. By 2012, it was between fifty and sixty. With the medications I was taking, my heart was slowing down.

After Christmas of 2012, I was watching the college bowl games while Cheryl was visiting a neighbor. I fell asleep on the sofa or at least I thought it was sleep. My heart paused. After about seven seconds, thankfully it started to beat again. When I raised my head, I was trembling, and I had wet my pants. I tried standing, but I soon realized something had changed. I gathered my medications together and called Mike Marable and my brother-in-law. Mike and Larry showed up at the same time. Mike had brought me a baby aspirin, and Larry came prepared to take me to the hospital.

I walked to the registration desk in my pajamas with my medications. I gave them a brief history and told them that I was to let someone know if anything ever changed.

Something had changed. They triaged me and rolled me away in a wheelchair getting the check in information as we proceeded to the ER. Two doctors attended me asking questions to eliminate a seizure or a stroke. I told them up front it was heart related. They agreed and sent me to the cardiac floor of the hospital.

I was hospitalized for a week and wore a heart monitor. At night my heart rate would drop to a pulse rate of thirty-nine. That combined with continuous atrial fibrillation with an irregular heartbeat sometimes caused a pause to occur for several seconds. At the last checkup appointment with Dr. Miller, he had mentioned that in the future I might be a candidate for a pacemaker or defibrillator.

Since my admission to the hospital, Dr. Murrow was the cardiologist making his rounds to see me every morning. I had been diagnosed as having bradycardia. After five days, he told me that they were taking this episode very seriously.

I told him I was glad they were, and as he was about to leave again without giving a prognosis, I blurted out, "Dr. Murrow, you do know that I had a partial node ablation?"

He stopped in midstride and looked me dead in the eyes. "You had a partial node ablation?"

I said, "Yes, sir, about twenty years ago, and the downside of that operation was supposed to be a pacemaker. So if you are hesitant about putting one in, I am ready to get it done and get out of here."

Looking me dead in the eye he said, "I tend to agree with you."

That afternoon I met Dr. Woodard. The next morning I received my pacemaker and was dismissed the next day. My heart rate was set to sixty beats a minute. I could check my watch and pulse at the same time. Though a steady sixty-pulse rate was much better than what I had been living with, it was not enough. I bounced back but not all at once and not far enough.

Since 1980, I had taken Coumadin. The laboratory drew a vial of blood every month and tested it for my clotting time. This was done in an effort to protect me against stroke. By 2015 I had successfully taken Coumadin for thirty-five years. I thought that had to be some kind of record.

I started to have, on occasions, a very slight swimmy head especially when I lay down. It did not seem to incapacitate me, and it was not painful. On September 23, 2015, I awakened at 6:00 a.m. to go to the bathroom with intentions of returning to bed. When I stood, I do not remember my feet ever touching the floor. I crashed head first into my closet knocking my entire wardrobe to the floor. The corner of the dresser inside the closet dug into my back. I got to my feet and called my primary care doctor, Dr. Gilbert.

His answering service connected me with the on call doctor. She advised me to go to Dr. Gilbert's sick call at 7:45 a.m. She thought I was suffering from vertigo. Dr. Gilbert confirmed her suspicions and gave me vestibular exercises to do to help with the condition. I followed his instructions, but after several days I was not any better and returned to see Dr. Gilbert. I thought my vision was worse, so he sent me to an eye specialist. It was late in the day when the retina specialist tested me, but the test was negative. I returned to Dr. Gilbert, and he sent me to a neurologist. He also diagnosed vertigo and sent me through the St. Mary's advanced vestibular program with their physical therapist. I made an appointment to see their therapist, but my condition worsened before I could make the appointment.

I was experiencing an altered gait and having balance issues. My depth perception was off. I took myself off the road and only drove when absolutely necessary. One of the necessary appointments was the lab work for Coumadin. Dr. Gilbert's nurse was attending me in the lab that day, and I told her that I thought Dr. Gilbert and the doctors were chasing the wrong rabbit, so to speak. She asked if I would like to see him again. I said yes, and she worked me in.

This time Dr. Gilbert asked some of the same questions as before but added, "How long have you been taking Coumadin?"

I said, "About thirty-five years."

He then commented that some patients taking anticoagulants for long periods of time develop slow bleeds and said, "But you haven't been having headaches."

I did not classify the pressure behind my eyes as pain. Nevertheless, he sent me to Athens Diagnostic for a CAT scan of my head. I could not have a MRI because of my pacemaker.

Consequently, the doctor at Athens Diagnostic read and verbally relayed to Dr. Gilbert that the CAT scan was normal. Apparently, the image was misread, and that prolonged the correct diagnoses. I continued to live with what I thought was a severe case of vertigo.

On Christmas Eve 2015, three months after my fall, I woke up with a sick headache. For the past thirty years we had always hosted

Cheryl's side of the family with a Christmas Eve dinner, and I had been the grill master.

As I made up my bed, the Lord spoke to me as clearly as he ever has. "If you don't take care of this, it is going to kill you."

I called out to Cheryl to cancel everything for Christmas Eve and drive me to the emergency room. Only one other person was in front of me at the registration desk. When the registrar had finished with that patient, she asked me what my problem was. The last thing I remember saying is, "I woke up this morning with a sick headache." I did not remember anything else until I woke up in the intensive care unit hooked up to life support and half out of my head.

The hospital ran another CAT scan of my brain. The doctors said I had twelve milliliters of blood between my cranium and my gray matter. That sounded more like the right diagnoses.

The neurologist explained to me on Christmas Day. "You have a choice. If we operate to remove the blood, one in four patients has to return to the hospital after being dismissed. If you stay long enough for your body to absorb the blood on its own, you most likely will not have to return."

I agreed to the latter. Five days later, the twelve milliliters was reduced to six and at ten days it was negligible. I was sent to rehabilitation for a period of time. My medications were adjusted, and I was taken off anticoagulants, but of course I became a very high risk for stroke. Once again, I was on the cutting edge of technology. At that time the Lariat procedure was all that could be done for patients that could not take anticoagulants. Apparently, patients were having negative repercussions with that procedure, so I opted for a second opinion.

I was discharged from the hospital on January 10, 2016, and immediately sought a second opinion.

Dr. Murray's office was a satellite office of the Emory Heart Clinic located in Athens, Georgia. I was impressed with his apparent qualifications. The walls of his office were literally covered with diplomas.

I estimated close to twenty framed documents. I complimented him. "How impressive!"

He graciously shrugged it off and started right away with the consultation.

On his computer he pulled up an image of a heart and pointed to the appendage that was the focus of the new procedure. He told me that 90 percent of all strokes in patients that have atrial fibrillation were caused by embolism of the blood trapped in the appendage. If the blood never found an entrance to the appendage, it would not become stringy. That would eliminate the risk of a stroke if it found its way out of the appendage. He had performed twenty successful procedures over the previous six months. By placing a clip over the entrance of the appendage, I would no longer be required to take anticoagulants. I agreed to have the procedure done.

He then started to ask me about my history. He specifically wanted to know if I had any previous injuries to my left rib cage and lung. I chuckled and told him about the wreck.

He listened intently and responded. "Well, I am going to have to collapse it again to be able to get the tools in place to clip the appendage."

I knew how difficult rehabilitation would be with oxygen treatments after being recently discharged from the hospital. I did not have all my strength back from the brain hemorrhage, but I could not risk waiting for my strength to return.

My operation was on January 22, 2016. The morning after the procedure, I awoke in my room with a large bandage under my left arm and, just below it, a one-half-inch tube was stuck through my ribs draining the fluid from my left lung. Dr. Murray and his assistants entered my room.

Dr. Murray said, "Let's see how that drainage is doing."

He was elated to see only slightly pinkish ooze in the clear tube.

Right away, he said, "We can get rid of this tube, and you can go home." He pulled the tube out and bandaged me up and called the discharge nurse.

The nurse gave me instructions and sent me home with oxygen. It took me a couple of months to shed the oxygen and two more months to get my strength back.

# On Medical Technology's Cutting Edge

On at least three different occasions since 1993, I have received the benefits of breakthroughs in modern medical technology: (1) the partial node ablation of the interventricular septum, (2) the clip of the left atrial appendage, and (3) a dual wired pacemaker. I resist the notion that I have just been lucky and tend to be grateful for these breakthroughs and consider them as blessings from God.

The third and most recent blessing came in the spring of 2017 as I started preparing my garden spot for planting. Mike Marable turns under my garden spot with his tractor and harrow each year, and I finish the soil preparation with a five-horsepower garden tiller. Unlike the previous years, I noticed how fatigued I was becoming after about five minutes behind the garden tiller. I pulled up a chair and rested for five minutes and plowed for five minutes.

I was also noticing the old nemesis of fluid retention. If I consumed too much salt, I would bloat easily and hear the wheezing in my lungs when I laid down. I could counter the symptoms by going on a strict diet, but that made me aware of how narrow the margin was from heart failure.

My routine pacemaker checkup was in May, so I told Dr. Woodard about my symptoms. He seemed to know right away what needed to be done. To confirm his suspicions, he gave me another echocardiogram to see if there had been any changes since the last echo four years earlier. There had been a significant change. I was suffering from severe mitral valve regurgitation.

Within the cardiology group, different cardiologists have their specialties. The valve expert in my cardiology group was Dr. Ben Holland. During his evaluation of my condition, he told me of several procedures short of open-heart surgery that might be in order for me. However, when closer and clearer images of my heart were taken, no less-invasive procedures could be performed on my heart. Because of the thirty-five years of heart disease, my heart was contorted in shape making the internal valve function close improperly and insecurely after each beat. It was looking more like open-heart surgery to replace the valve as the only answer, except for another breakthrough.

The FDA had approved a new dual wire pacemaker. Dr. Woodard was optimistic that if my old pacemaker were replaced with the newer model, the second wire would cause both sides of my heart muscle to squeeze in unison instead of the lag time created by only a single wire pacemaker. He believed the uneven contraction was causing the regurgitation. He was right!

I could tell the day after I received my new pacemaker that I was much better. They increased my pulse rate to seventy beats per minute. I felt splendid! Praise the Lord!

Dr. Holland and Dr. Woodard both informed me that the risk of invasive surgeries in the future would be based on how well I was feeling. Simply put, why risk painful surgery and long rehabilitation periods if it made me feel worse than the symptoms. After a follow-up echocardiogram, the mitral valve regurgitation was still significant but out of the heart failure range. At age sixty-eight, when I consider the progress made over the last twenty-seven years, I am truly thankful.

# Leaving the Legacy: It Can't Be Luck

America offers its citizens a level playing field to seek the American dream. Several factors play into the success or failure of that pursuit. Having been born in the United States was the first big advantage for my family and me as a child. The Christian influence from my immediate family's heritage of faith was another factor. The Christian influence from a community and extended family such as Antioch Christian Church, the oldest Christian denominational church in Georgia, was another.

There is a theme woven into the Christian faith, "Once saved, always saved." When I accepted Jesus Christ as my personal savior and Lord at the age of ten, I didn't know all of what it meant to be a Christian, but I would have a lifetime to find out.

All children under the age of accountability come under an umbrella of eternal protection from the Lord Jesus Christ. When an adolescent or an adult makes a personal decision to follow Jesus, effectively he or she has sealed their eternal destiny. Neither I nor anyone else understands all of what it means to be a Christian. That is the beauty of living a life of faith. The trickiest part of a Christian's journey through life may be learning to discern God's will and following his guiding light.

Though I have never been a perfect person and never will be, he has accepted me with all my faults. It has been his will to change me over my lifetime. It takes a willingness of believers to allow him to shape us as we give up more of ourselves to his will. By giving up our faulty nature, we never loose but become benefactors and heirs to countless blessings.

It would be terribly presumptuous and a horrible mistake to believe that my life without Christ could have resulted with the same joyous outcome as what my experiences has wrought. Knowing God has taken a lifetime. I will never fully know him until I am finally in his presence. What I do know about him—he is worthy of all the honor and glory that others and I can bestow upon him.

Learning his attributes helps tremendously in knowing him in an intimate and personal way. Within his infinite powers, holiness and love are the attributes of the great triune God. These attributes never conflict with one another. Though the span of a human lifetime seems like a long time to the one living it out, it is but a "flash in the pan" compared to eternity.

It is impossible to wrap our minds around his dispensation of grace, mercy, love, justice, wisdom, omniscience, omnipresence, etc. We cannot fully understand how an entity, a person so great, could have a personal relationship with a single human being such as we are, but in that same capacity he loves us more than we can know or understand. If we did totally know or understand his greatness, he would not be God to us.

We should always hope but never expect that we will live out an average life expectancy of seventy to eighty years or longer. There have been many young Christian lives taken home to be present with him. We belong to him, and he has bought us with the tremendous price of sacrificial love. Many parents are never prepared to let their children go back to the Creator because it is not the natural order. At any point during our Christian lives, we should be prepared always to leave on short notice.

During my life on no less than four occasions, I have walked through the valley of the shadow of death. However, I feared no evil to come to me. Each occurrence provided another testimony to his faithfulness. Instead of becoming a famous singing star, it became quite obvious to me that I had become a testimonial witness to his ever-abiding presence and protection. If I failed to praise him and give him the glory that he deserved, the rocks would cry out. What greater calling could a Christian have than this?

# Epilogue

After I was removed from the heart transplant list in 1992. I continued my appointments with the Emory Center for Heart Failure every six months until my retirement in 2013. With their expertise and the great maintenance medications I went without any heart failure symptoms for over twenty years. The evidence that my heart was wearing out first came with a diagnosis of bradycardia in 2013. I received my first pacemaker at that time.

For about two years the pacemaker helped but it was not the actual remedy. I noticed my fatigue increasing as I walked behind my garden tiller and there was some fluid retention at night. I brought this to the attention of Dr. Woodard of the Piedmont Cardiology Group. He explained that pacemakers were his area of expertise and referred me to the valve expert in the group, Dr. Ben Holland.

I was given another echocardiogram and it was discovered that my ejection fraction, on a scale from zero to sixty had slipped from above forty to around thirty-five and I was diagnosed with severe mitral valve regurgitation. Dr. Woodard explained he could help this by implanting a newly FDA approved dual wire pacemaker. When the wires were strategically placed in the heart muscle, he could make both sides of the muscle contract at the same time forcing more blood into the atrium. What Dr. Holland could do as the valve expert was to place a clip on the worn-out valve causing it to close more securely with each beat.

To gather more information, I was given an esophagus echocardiogram for a closer look inside my heart. The results of a life long battle with atrial fibrillation and congestive cardiomyopathy became evident. That is when I was told 'any further invasive surgery would be predicated on how well I was feeling.'

In May of 2018 the 1968 graduating class of Oconee County High School was celebrating their 50th year reunion. The Alumni Association had set forth an annual program involving each class reaching their 50th year. It would be their function to host all other classes with a banquet. I joined the 1968 committee in the planning for the 2018 banquet.

There were over two dozen classmates on the committee. I shared with the committee my precarious health situation but still was able to attend the meetings and the banquet in June. I kept them informed of my condition.

I returned to Dr. Woodard and he implanted the dual wire pacemaker just under the skin and that helped until 2018. In 2018 my teeth were breaking and cracking so I researched dental implants verses dentures. I decided to go with dental implants. That became very involved and required two surgeries under anesthesia to have my teeth removed and titanium rods were implanted in my cheekbones. In July of 2018 I also had a hernia operation.

The latter part of 2018 was difficult for me. I expected to bounce back to the level of normalcy I was experiencing before the three surgeries. The normalcy did not come. Fluid retention increased and my torso became tight to the touch and I was not sleeping well. After 24 years of maintenance I was once again in heart failure for a third time.

After Thanksgiving in 2018 I called the Piedmont Cardiology Group and asked for help. They immediately doubled my diuretics and the fluid started to come off and I rested much better. I was given two appointments within three days of the call. One was for an up to date echocardiogram. The other appointment was to go over the results.

I met with Dr. Holland again and he asked me, "How did we leave this last year?" I told him the cardiology group had decided that 'any further invasive surgeries would be predicated on how well I felt.' He resumed that train of thought with, 'because you would not have survived open-heart surgery at that time. He then said, "But, that was last year. This year the manufacturers have developed a clip that is the right size to work in your case. What do you think about that?" I gave him a literal thumbs up and he immediately stood and said, "Good! I will put you down for some time in March of 2019 but we may call you in sooner."

The preliminary requirements for the mitral valve clip procedure were (1) a pulmonary test, (2) a carotid artery check, (3) a meeting with the surgeon and (4) a right left heart catherization. When I met with Dr. Morris, the surgeon, we had an extensive conversation about my history and current condition. He told me that my heart was worn out and I had expressed my condition excellently and the group's main goal was to help me. He stopped in the middle of the meeting and said to me, "Let's take another look at that echo." He left the room to make a telephone call to Dr. Holland. I listened through the walls as best I could over the nurses chatter and other patients in the contiguous rooms. I heard him say to Dr. Holland that I was under the impression that I was too big of a risk to under-go open heart surgery but he did not consider me to be that big of a risk.

When he returned, he told me that I also had a tricuspid valve leak and it would only get worse with time. He also told me that if they performed the mitral clip procedure, it would hinder their ability to help me in the future. However, if I chose to have open-heart surgery, they could fix all of it and that might be the best alternative. The final preliminary check was the right/left heart catherization. I continued on with those steps since these preliminary requirements would be necessary no matter what I chose to do.

When the day of the right/left heart catherization came, Dr. Holland visited Cheryl and me just before the procedure. He reiterated what Dr. Morris had told me and encouraged me to give it serious consideration. He realized we would be changing directions and it was sudden but not an emergency situation. He said, "If you want to pump the brakes and get a second opinion, the Piedmont Cardiology Group would understand." That is what Cheryl and I decided to do. My right/left heart catherization went well. It had been twenty-four years since I had the first one. It was amazing to me to hear the exact same words Dr. Holland spoke immediately afterwards as being the identical words spoken to me after the first one twenty-four years prior, "Your coronary arties look great!" I had given consent for them to use stents if blockages were found while undergoing that procedure. The good news of no blockages simply meant the work that needed to be done was on the inside of my heart with primarily the valves. Dr. Morris also said that during the open-heart-surgery they could perform the Maze procedure and possibly remedy the atrial fibrillation that had plagued me my entire life.

I called Dr. Andrew Smith at the Emory Center for Heart Failure in Atlanta for a second opinion. Dr. Smith returned the call and we discussed my concerns. With my history I was hesitant to have my heart stopped to have it mended and wondered if it would start back up. Dr. Smith gave overwhelming approval of Dr. Morris's recommendation and after prayerful consideration I rescheduled an appointment with him to continue with open-heart surgery.

Cheryl and I went together for the meeting with Dr. Morris. He went over all that he wanted to do. He wanted to replace the mitral valve, repair the tricuspid valve and perform the Maze procedure. When he was finished and all our questions answered he asked, "When do you want to do it?" I said, "As soon as possible." To that response he said, "Come on." We walked to his nurse's station and he scheduled me for the next week, March 15, 2019. From that day forward my life was in the hands of God and the surgeons.

I remember going in on Friday morning of March 15 with my brother Jimmie. I remember very little from then until Sunday afternoon on the 17th as they said it would be. I can only add a delirious perspective to what occurred during those hours when I could not remember. Cheryl was with me during that period but I wasn't doing very well. As my numbers improved the doctors told Cheryl to go home and get some rest.

The spiritual bond between Cheryl and me as husband and wife is strong. Since my retirement, in the mornings when she is getting ready for work, I rise with her and make the coffee and bring it to her. I then go back to bed but strangely awaken as she drives down the driveway. I am not sure if in my spirit I sense her separation from me but it has happened too much to discount. Soon after she left the hospital to come home my numbers plummeted. The doctors apologetically called her back to the hospital saying they were sorry but I was unresponsive.

It saddens me to think of how that must have made my family feel at that moment. Nevertheless, by the time she arrived the Lord had set me on a rehabilitative course from a very low place toward the benefits of the extensive surgery that had been performed. I was so ready to leave the hospital I prayed to the Lord that I wanted his perfect timing with the removal of all the needles and tubes that were keeping me there. Almost immediately the medical personnel started removing them. It was amazing to see how God responded so quickly and completely when I turned it all over to him. I asked that same prayer for my rehabilitation.

As I write it has been sixty days since the surgery. I came home from the hospital after twenty-one days. I was released from home health care after thirty-one days. I had the last lung tube removed at thirty-eight days and I continue to work on my endurance levels without the use of oxygen. I am able to drive myself to and from my follow-up appointments. During the follow-up appointment with Dr. Woodard I mentioned Dr. Holland had said it could take up to a year before I noticed the benefits of the surgery. Dr. Woodard smiled and said, "Let's say by Christmas." Tomorrow I will see Dr. Holland. I have every reason to believe he will be in agreement with Dr. Woodard's evaluation.

As expected, my appointment with Dr. Holland went well. He is a very delightful and optimistic cardiologist. He wants to see me again in two to three months. Next week I will see Dr. Marty of the cardiology group. Until then Dr. Holland wants me to increase my activities but not over exert myself.

I have restricted my gardening to setting out a half-dozen tomato plants and a few pepper plants with the help from my good friend Gary Reynolds. I am considering cutting the grass with my Zero-Turn riding mower soon. I have obviously ignored my part of the yard work this spring. However, Cheryl has worked diligently from the patio out into the yard. The house, flowers, shrubs and grass look beautiful.

As I look back over my sixty-nine years of living it is plain for me to see that my wife and I have been tremendously blessed by God. Many men of my generation and my father's generation were not allowed to grow old but served God and Country in a capacity few other men would choose to do. Prayer has been a very significant part of my survival. I have a praying church, praying friends and an extended family that believes in the power of prayer. Having lived through the last half of the twentieth century and the first nineteen of the twenty first, I can see how God has blessed the marvels of medical technology. I have been the appreciative benefactor of those blessings. I hereby ascribe all the glory and honor to him and give thanks to him because I know, "It Can't be Luck."

*Billy Boyd Lavender*